America in the Modern World

America in the Modern World

D. W. BROGAN

LL.D., D. ès Lettres, F.B.A.

FELLOW OF PETERHOUSE AND PROFESSOR OF
POLITICAL SCIENCE IN THE UNIVERSITY OF CAMBRIDGE

RUTGERS UNIVERSITY PRESS
NEW BRUNSWICK   NEW JERSEY

Library of Congress Catalogue Card Number: 59-13541

Manufactured in the United States of America by
Quinn & Boden, Inc., Rahway, New Jersey

Designed by Leonard W. Blizard

To Nora Beloff

Preface

The substance of this book was delivered as lectures before Rutgers University in March, 1959. All I have done is to remove one or two local and temporary allusions from the text. Otherwise I have left the lectures exactly as they were delivered, denying myself the dangerous pleasures of hindsight. I have, however, added a brief epilogue, not with any intention of withdrawing anything I said but rather with the intention of stressing in a new context what I think to be the main message of these lectures.

I have to thank very warmly not only the long-suffering audiences to whom these lectures were delivered but the even longer-suffering staff of Rutgers University Press.

D. W. BROGAN

Cambridge
Armistice Day, 1959

Contents

America in the Modern World

1

A World They Never Made

"A world they never made." I am fully aware of the dangers inherent in applying to a people of one hundred seventy millions a poet's insight into personal psychology. And in beginning my discussion of the world in which the American people to their great discomfort find themselves, I am not professing to expound an exact or even an approximately verifiable science. I am attempting something both more humble and more bold, the calling of the attention of Americans to what I, a sympathetic foreigner but nevertheless a foreigner, think is the first cause of their discomfort, the first cause of the degree of suspicion, apprehension, bewilderment with which many, many Americans regard the world of 1959 and the world that they see lying beyond 1959.

To begin with, it is a world they never made. In making that judgment on the contemporary world the average American is not indulging in more than the usual human allowance of permissible shorthand. In one sense the United States is most decidedly one of the makers of the modern world; in some respects the United States is the chief maker of the modern world. But in the sense in which I am using the metaphor, the poet's insight, the world that the American today is forced to regard and fear is one that he feels little responsibility for making and little consequent capacity for understanding. Not only is it a world defying his sense of both what is reasonable and what is right. It is a world that somehow or other has replaced the other, better, happier, more harmless world that lay alongside the United States, in few relations with it but those relations friendly, hopeful, innocent.

The American does not like the world in which he finds himself (who does?), but he dislikes it the more because it has replaced a world that may indeed never have existed. It certainly did not exist in the simple innocent form in which the American tradition remembers it, but it was not totally mythical and had some if not all of the attractiveness that the tradition lends it. The American today, it seems to me, has slowly accepted the fact that this is a case of Paradise Lost, not just Paradise Mislaid, and naturally he laments his exile from Eden. Naturally he fears the flaming sword that sweeps between him and the innocent garden of his youth.

It is time, I am sure, to leave metaphor, to leave poetry, and to try to present in more prosaic terms the nature of the present dilemma that perplexes the American, the nature of some of the varying characteristics of the world in which the American has to live. What is the first that has to be stressed, the first American disillusionment?

It is, I think, the discovery that progress is an ambiguous term. All of us, or most of us, know that progress—the view that the world more or less inevitably and easily got better and better—is a novel idea in the history of the human mind. It seemed more natural until quite recently in our human story to look to the past, to a golden age in which mankind lived happily under the benevolent protection of the "laws of nature and of nature's God" for the epoch of human felicity. I do not know that at any time in past history mankind thought it was living in the golden age or even in the silver age. At best it was the age of iron that each generation saw itself embedded in. But in the past things were better till we paid for "the crude apple that corrupted Eve."

It was against this traditional pessimism of the human race, reflected in legend all over the earth, that the idea of progress—the idea that the present was better than the past, the future better than the present—was a protest and one that since, say, the late fifteenth century began to captivate the Western mind. To find the line of progress, to move along that line, to cooperate with the winning forces of destiny, to welcome with open hands the gifts of nature, given the more lavishly when those hands were capable of using and developing the gifts—these were the first duties of modern man. And if man did his duty he would be rewarded from a horn of plenty of an unprecedented size and generosity.

> The world's great age begins anew,
> The golden years return.

They return; but far more golden than in the past, for Shelley saw the future of the free man in the free society as much more attractive than the golden age of the Greeks. We stand on the shoulders of the ancients, said Bacon, and naturally we see farther and reach higher. I could multiply the citations but I need hardly do so. The theme is the commonplace of our Western tradition, finding some of its most eloquent expression in America in the Declaration of Independence, some of its most adroit and plausible exemplification in the writings and achievements of Franklin. "He snatched the lightning from heaven, and the sceptre from tyrants." So wrote Turgot of the American who, as politician and technological innovator, best justified American hopes at the birth of the American Republic. Franklin, Jefferson, the names say a lot.

But more important than the great names of great men is

a fact about American life that I want to emphasize now and shall have occasion to emphasize again. It was not only the great Americans who believed in progress, it was all Americans. This country was born in the age of progress, baptized in the religion of progress, created and peopled by men and women who believed in progress, in some amelioration for themselves, in more for their children; it was in hope as well as in resentment and rebellion that they had crossed the Atlantic to a new world that, often unconsciously, they knew they had to make and resolved, again often unconsciously, to make better. Many attempts have been made, some of them profound and just, to characterize the American people. Surely one of their marks, until very recent times, has been that they have been a people of hope, of believers in amelioration. They have been a people for whom the bonds of tradition have not been allowed to justify inertia, the acceptance of visibly inferior conditions simply because that was the way of the fathers.

This hopefulness of the American view of life can be illustrated in many ways. Professor Perry Miller has shown us how the early American Calvinists, grim, fatalistic, pessimistic as they may seem, as they must seem to preachers of "togetherness," were in fact by the standards of seventeenth-century Europe optimistic, ill-disciplined, cheerfully inconsistent. With them, as with Dr. Johnson's would-be philosopher friend, "cheerfulness would keep breaking in." The new world offered new possibilities and "no man who had been born in Boston needed to be born again."

It would be possible to cast shadows on this picture. The greatest of Americans, that is, the man I consider the greatest of Americans, had a strong streak of pessimism in his nature. As much as Dr. Reinhold Niebuhr, Lincoln had a sense of man's essentially tragic situation. So it is expressed in that great but not 100 per cent American document, the Second Inaugural; so it is revealed in Lincoln's quotation from *Mac-*

beth at the moment of his triumphant return from captured Richmond:

> Duncan is in his grave;
> After life's fitful fever he sleeps well.

But the greatest men of a nation are too great to be fully or merely representative and the representative American has, until recently, seen the story of the human race as on the whole a success story and one part of it as undoubtedly a success story, the history of the United States, the creation here, on this continent, of the last, best hope of earth. And if melodramatic pessimism is a luxury Americans could allow themselves because they did not really doubt that theirs was a success story, the pessimism that I seem to note today is not merely melodramatic; it is real, alarmed, and shows for the first time a realization that the human story may go wrong, that the old pessimistic cyclical theory of human destiny may be the true one—and that the American people are inextricably involved in the common, dangerous, and only intermittently hopeful destiny of the human race. For the American is beginning to realize that he can neither remake the world according to the American plan (for many Americans, necessarily God's plan) nor contract out. If the human race would obey or imitate, all would be well soon, if not now. But the hope of obedience or imitation is weak if not dead.

This, it seems to me, is the first ground for American discontent and alarm. The world is not visibly going the American way and is still less visibly content to let the Americans go their way, "the world forgetting, by the world forgot."

What were the American hopes that have been shattered? The first is that the United States having made herself by her exertions would save the world by her example. How deep that faith was, how justified, a cursory glance at history abundantly illustrates. In an international as well as in a national sense, America had erected a standard to which all good men could and, it was confidently believed, *would* repair. It was not for nothing that the founders of the Republic adopted a proud Latin motto: "Novus ordo seclorum," a new order of the ages. (You will find this device on one of the three sacred documents of the Republic: not on the Declaration, not on the Constitution, but on the dollar bill).

In a world still sunk in tyranny, empty tradition, political and religious servility, the new Republic shone, free from the sins of the past, bright with the greatest hopes known in the upward history of man-upward, for no one, in America at least, doubted that, as an American poet was to put it with great effect if bad Latin, the banner with the strange device bore the inspiring motto "excelsior." It is easy to make fun of the poem, of the poet, of the sentiment, but to do so is to sin against the spirit of America—and to fail to understand both the greatness of the hopes and the present chill of the fears.

It was not a matter of mere national pride or conceit. The virtuous republic of Washington was a model, not a mere pattern laid up in heaven but taking form in the remote American forest. The very hostility of conservative thinkers like de Maistre was proof of the fascination of the new state and the new society. Hopes dashed by the course of the French Revolution came to life again as the mild rule of Washington and then of Jefferson was contrasted with the Reign of Terror and the baleful, cometlike career of Napoleon. The great news was out; a free and orderly society could be created and mankind had far more hope of happiness open to him than had, until this happy day, been dreamed of. Again I could multiply the instances, from the repentance of his early hostility by William Cobbett to Goethe's famous praise of the new society:

Amerika du hast es besser.

But chronology supplies the most adequate example. It is a hundred years since the most profound and permanently valuable foreign commentator on the American scene and the American system died. And one of the lessons that Alexis de Tocqueville wanted to teach Europe—and especially France—was that the possibilities of human happiness, if not of exceptional human achievement, were greater than Europeans, especially conservative Europeans regretting the old order that America condemned by her success, had ever admitted to be possible. That way the Western world was going and that way, drab or dull as it might be, the greatest happiness of the greatest number lay.

On that shining picture a most ominous shadow lay—slavery. So the Civil War was both the punishment of American sin and the justification of faith in America. The victory of the North was a triumph for the cause of human freedom and dignity and John Bright, addressing a great meeting in favor of extending the franchise, interrupted his oration to give out the simple but meaningful message, "Richmond has fallen." So Walt Whitman was hailed by Swinburne; so all liberal Europe (including that semirepresentative figure, Karl Marx) welcomed the triumph of the Union. And the victors felt—and rightly felt—that this triumph not only was theirs but was the most manifest proof that faith in human progress and in a kindly destiny for mankind was justified.

That faith was naïve, so naïve that a quite different triumph, that of Bismarck's Prussia, was welcomed as a victory for the same good cause and the unification of Italy was welcomed both because national unity was a good thing and because it meant a decline, perhaps a fatal decline, in the power of Giant Pope. And the homage of imitation and admiration was not confined to statesmen and poets. It was made more manifest in the floods of immigrants who poured in, the greatest folk movement of which we have any adequate record. The Statue of Liberty was no more eloquent of America's role in the upward spiral of mankind than was Castle Garden and then Ellis Island. Every immigrant was a vote for America and the American way of life. It is my belief that the memory of this golden day still colors the American attitude toward the outside world and that some of the average American's discontent with that outside world springs from a deep regret that those days of automatic leadership for all the advancing peoples of the world seem to be over. They have of course been over for a long time. It was pointless to stress the sentiments of the poem of Emma Lazarus when the United States no longer welcomed the poor and the oppressed in the old, generous and, if you like, reckless way. Moreover, as Socialist criticism of the capitalist order grew in strength in Europe, the determinedly un-Socialist economy and political system of the United States became a stumbling block, a stone of offense to the makers and shakers of Europe. The United States became less the country that had freed the slaves than the country that had hanged the Chicago anarchists, less the country of Lincoln than of the Standard Oil Company. And it was not only on the Left that the American image lost some of its dazzling brilliance.

The success story of Bismarck's Germany to some degree offset the success story of the United States. If it was Commodore Perry who forced the Japanese to go to school, they went to school at least as much to Prussia as to the United States or to Britain. Nor was this the only disillusionment. The formal imitation of American constitutional methods in Latin America gave only ambiguously gratifying results. The innocence with which Louis Kossuth had been hailed after the failure of the Hungarian rising of 1849 was hard to recapture when the finally triumphant Magyars turned out to be oppressors themselves.

The innocent, egalitarian farmer's republic had become the greatest industrial power in the world with all the problems of social order and justice that this dangerous promotion involved. America was virtuous; America was right;

America was promises; but America was not quite so innocent, not quite so conscious of deserved and spontaneous admiration.

The year 1914 was, it is now easy to see, the watershed. Then began our dangerous, disorderly, unpredictable world. Then the faith in automatic progress received its first, perhaps its greatest, blow. Yet to the innocent American, on the farm, in the corner store, in the White House, the lesson of 1914 seemed plain. America had it better; the murderous quarrels of Europe had not been and should not be exported. America should stay above the battle and with malice toward none should only step in to bind up the nations' wounds. Such was the high ambition of the most famous New Jersey statesman, and who can think that Woodrow Wilson was wrong in his first ambition, which was to be a mediator and not a victor? It is not my place to discuss or decide why that ambition failed and Wilson had to combine the two so different roles of being the head of a victorious coalition and the creator of a just and lasting peace. My purpose is to remind you that the Wilson of the last months of 1918, the first months of 1919, was the last American to revive in Europe (and outside Europe) the old faith in the good faith, the healing power, the moral superiority of the United States. With him there crashed a faith that has never been fully restored.

And that crash was all the more important because a new and baleful star had arisen, for surely the most important result of the First World War was not the Russian Revolution, that might have come anyway, but the Bolshevik Revolution, which I believe was made possible only by the war—and by the Allied victory, for that saved the Bolsheviks from destruction by the Germans.

The Russian Revolution is so much one of the turning points in world history that I need do no more than remind you of the fact, but the point I want to stress is that it had, among other results, one highly relevant for our purpose, the setting up of a rival and deeply hostile center of attraction to that still exercised by the United States.

In 1919 the American people made a desperate and totally hopeless effort to return to the peace that they had known yesterday. How quickly the crusading fervor wore off! How soon it was implausibly asserted that all American policy need do was to reverse the sins and errors of 1914-1919! Let America mind her own business; let her remember in a phrase of President Coolidge's (that may have been misunderstood) that "the business of the United States is business." Much could be said about this policy, if that it can be called. But it had one fatal fault. It ignored the fact that the world of 1919 was a world that owed its shape very largely to the power and policy of the United States. That policy may have been an error, that power may have been wrongly asserted, but the fact was there. The new and disillusioning world that the American people turned their back on was a world in whose making the American people had had a great share. For the sin of 1914 the innocent Republic had had no share of guilt. For the world of 1919-1939 the Republic, still in its own estimation innocent, had if not guilt at least a share in its creation.

Nothing could be further from my intentions than to indict American policy or the American people. It is easy to see how tempting it was to withdraw from the sinful outer world and to give only such leadership as was compatible with formal irresponsibility. But America had a share in the responsibility for the destruction of the hopes of 1919. Just before the outbreak of the second war an intelligent Frenchman, said that *all* the great powers involved—Britain, France, Germany, Russia, America—had committed enough sins, positively and negatively, to account for the disastrous state of the world. Perhaps the sins of the United States were mainly negative, but sins there were. But the American people did not see it in that light. They saw a series of undeserved slurs, a mass of undeserved hate, a degree of unprecedented ingratitude descend on the innocent Republic. They saw, with bitterness, what had happened to democracy in the world that they had hoped to make safe for it. They forgot, as Chesterton said at the time, that the world could not simply be made safe for democracy, for it is a dangerous trade.

Yet the contrast between impoverished Europe and booming America, if it fed hatred, envy and malice, also bred reluctant admiration. Europe, even the Soviet Union, was ready to go to school to the masters of them that knew. André Siegfried declared that the world would have to choose between Gandhi and Henry Ford, and in a more material, less ideologically impressive fashion the United States was for a brief moment, again, the last best hope of earth. Then came the catastrophe from which, in my opinion, American prestige has not fully recovered and whose reverberations still weaken her world position.

It is again far from my intention to assess responsibility for the smash of 1929 or for the long and slow haul of the American economy out of the slough of despond into which the American people were plunged and in which they, in a sense, remained until the coming of the Second World War. What I am concerned with is the impact on the outer world and the rebounding of that impact on the American view of the outer world.

It seems to me to matter little whether Europe made the smash or whether the United States pursued its own destruction. Seen from the outside, what mattered was that the great exemplar of a liberal economy had failed, that the policy of abundance had failed, that the secret of high wages (as it had been optimistically described) had been lost.

The decline in European faith in the American political way of life that had occurred so precipitately in 1919-1920 was followed by an equally precipitate decline in faith in the American economic way of life. All the radical, Socialist fear and suspicion of American capitalism was revived; it was reinforced, made more formidable by the rise of communism, now the doctrine, the political weapon of a great state. Everywhere democratic values plummeted down like so many overpriced stocks. In the crash the feeble new democratic institutions and habits of Germany and Japan were smashed as the feeble democratic institutions of Italy had been smashed in the previous decade. Whether on the Left or on the Right, the day seemed to be to the authoritarian way of life. The answer lay not in free cooperation but in some form or other of dictatorship. True, in the first years of the New Deal the spectacle of a democratic leader taking the initiative was a refreshing novelty. But the successes of the New Deal were limited and not easily imitable in countries with less abundant resources. Franklin D. Roosevelt remained a symbolic leader in a world of dictators or of drab and timid parliamentary chiefs like Chamberlain and Daladier, but the American people were too committed to isolation for him to do more than exemplify principles and moral passions. He could advise; he could not lead, even if he had been determined to lead—which it is not quite certain that he was.

The world that drifted to war or was rapidly pushed to war (I think the latter is the truer view) was a world for which the United States, by her immediate past and by her power, had a great responsibility but in which her role was played ineffectually and evasively. As far as the second war was "the unnecessary war," as Sir Winston Churchill was later to call it, the main fault for not avoiding it must fall on the rulers—and peoples—of Britain and France. But there is some American share to be noted and I am convinced that much of the faith that the American people later put into the United Nations came from a sense of inadequacy and guilt in the recent past.

In the Second World War the role of the United States was curiously reversed. In the first war the American material contribution, although decisive, was limited in time and extent. In the second it was immense in time, in extent, in impact. It can be justly said that only for the United States was the Second World War truly a world war, that the United States alone threw her massive power into all theaters of war and that power was an indispensable condition of victory in all parts of the globe. It is true that the United States did not suffer as much as Russia or Britain—not to speak of Germany. But the world had an unforgettable lesson in the realities of American power. That lesson has not been forgotten.

On the ideological side the picture is not quite so impressive. True, President Roosevelt had difficulties to face that did not face President Wilson. He had an ally in the Soviet Union as embarrasing, at times, as the czardom would have been to Wilson had it survived. The very violence of the defiance of the democratic dogma by Nazi Germany was a kind of handicap. Imperial Germany and Republican America had more in common than had the Third Reich and the United States, and whether the policy of "unconditional surrender" was a mistake or not it was a natural mistake. But for these and other reasons, some personal and some political, the United States in the Second World War was not the admitted and solitary center of an ideological crusade. It was not in F.D.R.'s power, adroit orator as he was, to stir the masses of the world as Wilson had done and perhaps Wilson's successor was too conscious of Wilson's mistakes and Wilson's fate to wish to imitate him. Then death came before Roosevelt's policy was tested, before he could use the fund of good will and trust that he had accumulated.

Whatever the reasons, the United States in 1945 stood rather on a pinnacle of material power than on a peak of political leadership. Nothing in a sense was further from the minds of the American people than a desire to mount the peak of leadership. Innocently, the American people knew that they had won and deserved victory and believed that they had won, as they had deserved, peace. The new United Nations, the amicable continuance of wartime relations with the Allies (of whom the cunning British were as much to be feared as the rude Russians), would deal with the urgent questions. Meantime the American people could busily beat swords into plowshares or their equivalent and resume the slow upward climb to the old prosperity that had been temporarily lost. That climb proved easier and quicker than had been feared. What proved harder was the seeking of peace and the ensuring of it.

There was no question in 1945 of the United States not being a maker of the world of 1945. If the American public underestimated the difficulty and the duration of the task that fell on it, it did not for a moment deny that it had a share and a responsibility for the state of the world and for its salvation. Indeed, one of the most remarkable and comforting and creditable signs of the maturity of the American people has been found in the fact that no challenge put to them since 1945 has found them wanting in either generosity or courage. Even wisdom has been in more abundant supply than veterans of 1919 might have feared.

But it was soon found that virtue and good will were not enough. For one thing, they were supposed to call out equivalent virtues in other people and they did not conspicuously do so. The liberated and saved countries of Western Europe were barely capable of mere survival. The great power of Eastern Europe, in its most desperate need, yet preferred power to plenty and showed neither will to true accomodation of interests nor capacity to understand the real roots of American policy.

There were faults on both sides, faults committed during the war and after the war. But in 1947, contemplating the world around it, the American people, whatever their grievances against the foresight or lack of it of their rulers, could truthfully acquit themselves of any desire to exploit victory or to impose their will. If they preached and in a sense practiced and imposed democracy in Germany and Japan, they did so in good faith and in no spirit of revenge. If they were disappointed in their efforts, the disappointments were often taken philosophically or humorously. *The Teahouse of the August Moon* was a fable applicable in more places than Okinawa. On the whole, the results of American leadership and munificence in both Germany and Japan gratified the American people, who took possibly too complacent a view of their success as re-educators.

It was elsewhere that the American public suffered its great disillusionment and had fostered in it that attitude of resentful wonder at the outside world that is part of the American problem today. First of all, America was faced with the paradox not merely of ingratitude but of wrongly directed gratitude. It was not only that so many millions in France, in Italy, in Britain even, did not sufficiently appreciate what they owed to American power and generosity. It was that they felt or professed to feel more gratitude to the remote Soviet Union that had no doubt been a main force in bringing down the Nazi power but had not freed Paris or Rome from the Nazi forces or London from the daily menace of V-1 and V-2.

I shall certainly make no attempt to justify this error of morals and of judgment. Nor can I do more than allude to some reasons for it. All of Europe was exhausted, morally as well as physically debilitated, and full of more or less conscious resentment of the apparent prosperity and immunity of the United States. The contrast between New York and London in 1947 was dramatic enough for anyone who went to America frequently. To those who only knew of the earthly paradise by report it was humiliating, maddening or inexplicable. Or it was explicable simply. The Americans had taken the chance of the war vastly to enrich themselves. And they could only have done that at the expense of their allies. The old sullen Socialist suspicion of American capitalism revived. The contrast between the austerity of England, the gross inequalities of well-being in France and Italy, and what was rumored of the paradise over the ocean was more than human nature could bear. What the Americans had they owed to others. It was their duty, their interest to share it. Instead of being grateful for such acts of generosity as the Marshall Plan, Europeans should rather praise themselves for their magnanimity in letting the Americans do their duty! In this period I more than once recalled Napoleon's explanation of why the brothers and sisters whom he had made kings and princes were so ungrateful. "They think I have cheated them of their due share in the inheritance of our father the late King." So much of Europe felt regarding the plenty and the bounty of the United States.

It would be wrong to attach too much importance to this European attitude (which was far from universal) or to the natural American resentment of it. The Marshall Plan succeeded; Western Europe was saved from ruin and from communism and if the rescued were not adequately grateful or adequately conscious of the abyss from which they had been saved, the Americans were and are a pragmatic people. They had done what they set out to do and, although it would have been nice to be thanked for it, success is better than gratitude. And if the European nations by 1950 were in a position to answer back and be sassy, that was proof of the success of American policy. Like the parent of a troublesome teen-ager, the American as taxpayer and voter felt a mixture of pride and annoyance. But pride predominated.

But it was not in Europe that the average American was most disappointed. It was in Asia; it may soon be in Africa. It would be absurd to attempt to allocate praise or blame for the events in China, sometimes summed up in a misleading shorthand phrase as "the loss of China." But nothing is more natural or more defensible than the spontaneous American reaction to the discovery that China had been saved from Japanese imperialism only to fall under Communist control. I have always thought that the American interest in China owed more to missionary than to economic connections; nevertheless, the interest in China was deep and genuine.

There were few Pacific isolationists and it can plausibly be asserted that it was not only formally but really the determination to protect the "freedom of China" that brought America into the Second World War. Seeing China pass under Communist control, seeing the uprooting of a century of missionary effort, the quenching of a century of missionary hopes was an embittering and a blinding experience. It blinded many Americans to the fact that there are more than three Chinese for each American and no natural law determines that the United States can or could determine the fate of China. To "lose China" was to lose something that had never been possessed. Yet the sense of loss was reasonable and human, the sense of danger is not totally unreasonable now, and possibly will be much less unreasonable in the future.

If China is to be communized, transformed, deprived of its ancient weaknesses as well as its ancient virtues, this may be a greater event in the history of the world than even the Russian Revolution and one removing a great part of the human race from the American influence and leadership so confidently counted on in 1945. Here the American paradox is most bitter. For it was American victory, by eliminating Japanese power, that made possible the Communist victory in China. To have dropped the atomic bomb, to have risked that guilt, to produce such a result, this is irony unbearable. This is a world that no American wished to make but for which the United States must take some responsibility. If the American sense that the world is uncontrollable, not subject to reason and not necessarily moving in the direction of liberty and human betterment, has any one root it is in the great deception of China.

That deception was reinforced by the experience of the Korean War. To the average American, no war could be more innocent in origin, more worthy in object. Yet it was a war full of disillusionment. It involved a temporary but humiliating American defeat at the hands of those Chinese who had already inflicted a political defeat on the United States by their conquest of the Nationalists. Fought in the name of the United Nations, it was a war whose burden fell overwhelmingly on the Americans and for most of the members of the United Nations the motto was obviously "Let Sam do it." And it was a war settled in an unsatisfactory way.

Americans brought up to believe in what I once called "the illusion of American omnipotence" found it painful to accept and hard to believe that a settlement could mean less than a complete American triumph. Was it for this that tens of thousands of Americans had died in Korea as, before them, hundreds of thousands had died in the Pacific? This was a world unintelligible to millions of honest men and women. It was natural that they should seek an explanation in cries of "treason." And if that was not enough, there was the further resource of seeing a world in which the United States alone did its duty, and if that world was in a bad way the fault lay entirely elsewhere.

Nor was this the only disillusionment. It was natural to

see in the newly liberated nations children eager to come to school to the great pioneer in the cause of freedom, the great exemplar of the more abundant life. Yet everywhere eager pupils went to another school, not only in China but in other parts of Asia and Africa. The ending of the old imperialism did not necessarily give the United States a set of friendly, grateful, and admiring pupils. At most it gave the opportunity to compete in what often seemed a rigged market for the friendship and tolerance of the newly liberated peoples. It was even a shock to learn that in some liberated countries, like India, the old masters preserved in some minds more prestige than the new allies.

Far from finding a world ready to follow the American lead, the American people found, even in Latin America, a world that was ready to shop and bargain and hesitate as to which of the rival world leaders to follow. And even when the American people won the support or docility of the governments where the competition for adherence was keenest, it did not follow that they had won the most active elements of the population. To their horror and usually to their justified horror the American people found the tag of "imperialist" pinned to the coattails of Uncle Sam, and in the war for men's minds the American way did not always win. The old identification of liberty in the sense of freedom from foreign rule with liberty in the sense of freedom from domestic tyranny was no longer firm or even customary.

All over the world liberty in the first sense warred with liberty in the second, a war that was often waged to the loss of the United States, which offered not authoritarian leadership but the more complicated way to self-rule. Were the common peoples of the world so blinded by nationalist passion, so ill-equipped to work democracy, American style, that the United States must give up the old hope of being automatically the natural leader of nations rightly struggling to be free? That there should be any question, that there should be any contest between so obviously tyrannical a system as Russian communism and the time-tried and inevitably beneficent system proclaimed to a candid world in 1776 was an affront to the spirit of '76 and to the American belief in an intelligible and manageable world.

And when, in addition to the too often successful competition offered by new societies that prostituted the name of freedom and democracy, there was suddenly flashed across the heavens proof that the other competition in material achievement was open too, the American whose history had been so fortunate, who until this century and until this generation, had never had to consider the limits of American power, was forced to reconsider his national situation. At the moment when mankind was on the edge of adventuring into space, the old, familiar world seemed less familiar, less homely, more in danger of self-destruction than ever. And now it could no longer be doubted by even the most obstinate that of that old, dangerous, and ill-ordered world the United States was at last and finally a part. It is a world the Americans never made but have to live in.

2

The Challenge to American Democracy

I have already tried to explain some of the unease with which the American contemplates the world in which he has to live in terms of his bewilderment at the ending of the automatic progress of the human race in the right, that is, in the American, direction. I shall now try to develop that theme in one particular direction, to discuss the present position, the present efficacy, the present appeal of the American way of political life—what is for convenience called "American democracy." It is challenged; its premises are denied; it is in competition—willing or unwilling does not really matter—with another system calling itself "democratic," as well as with systems that without denying they are "democratic" do not stress their "democracy" so much as their "liberty." The American democracy is in a contest, which I think will certainly last my lifetime, with two forces, communism and authoritarian nationalism. This is a contest that it is not absolutely certain to win; certainly it is not likely to win if it makes no effort and takes no thought.

I should like to begin by limiting the use I am going to make here of the term "democratic." This word can be legitimately used in more than one sense, but the use I intend—and the one that I think most legitimate—is the political use. This use is implied in the assertion that all governments derive their "just powers from the consent of the governed," that the object of political society is the facilitating of "life, liberty, and the pursuit of happiness." It is the use that has for its guiding principle healthy skepticism—the two previous principles are examples of healthy faith—the doubt that any man or group of men can long be trusted with unlimited, uncontrolled power.

Democracy, as I interpret it, is the maximizing of the area of uncoerced choice and the chief instrument for that maximization is the political system, agreeing in principle if differing in detail, that has been until this century identified with liberal progress in Britain, in France, in the United States. That system was spreading rapidly and apparently efficaciously in 1914 and was seemingly destined to a universal triumph in 1918. That system is now under attack, is on the whole in retreat, and yet it is the system to which the United States is totally committed. A defeat of that system is a defeat for the United States; every extension of that system is a victory for the United States and a measure of increased security for the American people. To challenge that system is to challenge the American way of life at its most sensitive and most vulnerable spot.

The challenge takes two forms. In one form it is a simple contest for spheres of influence and for what, to use an old-fashioned term, may be called the balance of power. For instance, it is obviously in the interest of the United States that India should remain "democratic" in this general sense, even if the Indian form of democracy is modeled on the English rather than the American plan and even if Indian democracy differs greatly and (if you like) for the worse from both the English and the American plan. It would be dangerously pedantic to look abroad at the world and, where one could not find an exact working copy of the American constitution and the American political system, to write off that defective "democracy" as unworthy of interest and of support. Many objections could be made to the adoption of so haughty an attitude; the decisive one is that if it were adopted the United States would find itself alone in the world with no friends and lots of enemies.

In this contest, in the reply to this challenge, the United States will have to settle for a good deal less than perfection, a good deal less than loyal imitation. To the realities of that competition, the minimum conditions of fit membership in the "democratic world," I shall return later.

There is another challenge at least as important as that of the competition for the political leadership of the world or of a great part of it. There is the internal challenge, the challenge that the times with their new needs and their desperate dangers present to both the theory and the practice of the American constitutional system. Franklin D. Roosevelt spoke of the practices of a "horse-and-buggy age." Are these practices adequate for the age of Sputnik and Lunik? Is the spirit of '76 and the constitutional mechanism of 1789 adequate for an age in human history in which it is highly likely that many in this audience will live to see man successfully leave his tiny planet and adventure in outer space?

It is not merely a matter of how the American system impresses the outer world, but of how it works inside and outside the United States. It is not a matter of continuing to hold on to the prestige of the American way of life, of the American version of political democracy. It is a matter of assessing the political machinery of the United States in an epoch which one can truthfully say is unprecedented in human history. If Franklin and Jefferson could believe in a "new order of the ages" in 1776, what slogan is adequate for our world trembling on the edge of self-inflicted annihilation and of the conquest of outer space?

I should like to begin by making a profession of political faith. I hold that the existence of a political system, its duration, its roots in a fairly distant past are, if not proofs, at least indications that the political system has substantial merits. Survival is both a virtue and a proof of virtue. I could conceive of a system of government so visibly evil and with its evil so untainted by good that its survival could be explained only in terms of tyranny of the most ruthless and crushing kind, in the terms that George Orwell suggested in *1984*. I can conceive a "brave new world" of conditioned morons run by a handful of alphas for their own private and, to our thinking, intolerable ends. I have slightly more fear of Aldous Huxley's political hell than of George Orwell's. But I am not overwhelmingly afraid of either. To be frank, I think that some of the formidable strength of the Soviet Union and of Communist China comes from their virtues, not their sins, and that we shall disastrously deceive ourselves if we think otherwise.

To survive, to become a habit, these are the essentials of good government, even of tolerable government. They may not be enough. The political structure may be an impediment to much greater human felicity, revolution may be justified and, in rarer cases, essential. We should always remember that one good custom can corrupt a world. But this at least is my belief: these cases are rare. To be accepted and to be treasured are indications if not final proofs that a government is a success.

The relevance of these preliminary considerations to the position of the United States is obvious. It can truthfully be said that the government of the United States today is the oldest, the least changed in the world. It has endured, little changed formally and not profoundly changed in reality, for one hundred seventy years. Begging your tolerance I shall fall back on a historical parallel that I have used before. When George Washington took the oath as the first President of the United States he was beginning the tenure of a unique office. There were republics in the world then, most of them doomed to disappear in the great tempest of the French Revolution. But no Doge of Venice or Stadtholder of Holland was a republican magistrate of the kind that General Washington set out to be—the elected head of a state openly based on the free choice of the citizens, based not on tradition or habit but on a brand-new constitution that implied principles which for by far the greatest part of the world were blasphemy and treason.

When Washington took the oath in Wall Street there was a Son of Heaven in Peking as well as an impotent and cloistered Mikado in Kyoto. There was a completely autocratic Czarina in St. Petersburg and there was an autocratic King of France and Navarre doomed soon to lose throne and head alike. There was a King of Great Britain with a good deal of power exercised in intervals of sanity. There was a Sultan of Turkey who was also Caliph. There were tribal chiefs and theocratic states like Tibet and Rome. What was missing was the idea of political democracy, the habit of regarding government as a matter of choice by the people and not of obedience by the people to a ruler chosen directly or indirectly by God.

Is it not a matter for wonder that one hundred seventy years later, when nearly all these rival institutions have disappeared almost from living memory, the government of the United States still stands so little changed that the office held by General Eisenhower is far more like that held by General Washington than that held by Queen Elizabeth II is like that held by George III, not to speak of Elizabeth I?

Nor is that government imposed on the people or barely tolerated by it. The European visitor is impressed by many things in America, but often is most impressed by something that is not there: by the absence of a sizable, serious body of opinion that questions the legitimacy, the merits of the existing social and political system, that is ready to make all things new and finds in the existence of old institutions not a proof of virtue but a call to destruction and to reconstruction.

An eminent French priest, Father Bruckberger, a hero of the Resistance and conscious of the necessary harm done to French stability and unity by some of the methods and claims of the Resistance, has noted and envied this profound conservatism of the American people. In a world of dangerously rapid change, where the landmarks of today are washed away overnight and the landmarks of yesterday are antiques, like the statue of Ozymandias in the desert, this stability is something to be admired as well as wondered at.

Nor is this all. Under these piously preserved institutions the American people have grown and flourished in power, well-being, wealth, and civilization with a speed again unprecedented in history. If we are to judge a political system by its apparent fruits, the American system is fully justified and the American who thinks that little or nothing needs changing can say with Vergil:

Sic fortis Etruria crevit.

Thus and in no other way did the United States become great.

I have already made plain my acceptance in general of this devotion to the American way of organizing political life. That the United States has flourished under that system cannot be doubted, that the loyalty of the American people to their institutions is an immense asset cannot be doubted by one who, like myself, has had to travel and live in a postwar Europe where the visible cracks in the political superstructure suggest the alarming possibility of still graver fissures in the foundations. If the American people are, in general, content with their institutions they are right to be content. Political stability and political loyalty are too precious goods to be risked for any mere passion for modernity or for political sophistication.

But in the world competition in which, willy-nilly, the United States is entered there are dangers in this complacency. To begin with, there is the danger of transferring to our age the general prestige and power of attraction that American institutions won and held a century ago. A modern Tocqueville contemplating the world might be less certain than the first Tocqueville that the future was to the American way. He took Russia seriously enough as a rival pole of power but not as a rival pole of attraction. Today he would have to consider the possibility that the Russian way to power and even to abundance, if not to freedom, might prove to a great part of the world not only as attractive but more practicable than the American way. That long decline in the traditional prestige of American institutions which I tried earlier to trace in outline has had as a consequence the awkward fact that American institutions are no longer finding a seller's market. At best they are just able to make their merits appreciated in a highly competitive market.

It is this external challenge that so many Americans find hard to understand. Can there be nations so dead to the truth, to all common sense, to the universal rules of morals as not to accept, at once, the superiority of American democracy and the bogus character of systems that take the name democratic only the better to deceive and to betray? The American who has never asked himself any questions about the justification of the American way of political life, who conceives of democracy only in American terms, who has no adequate notion of the historical environment in which, so far, American democracy has been a shining success, who consequently has no notion of the fragility of the achievement, is—once out of his native environment—often a victim to hostile propaganda.

The distressing discovery that American soldiers in Korea

were more susceptible to seduction than were the Turks should have provoked more critical reflection than it did. If they had ever been allowed or encouraged to consider the possibility that all was not well with the American political system, if they had been given better and more dignified reasons for fighting for America than its superiority in the number of washing machines or in the size of cars, brainwashing might not have been so easy. Just as the child of a rigorously orthodox family, brought up sheltered from the truth that many people do not share his religious beliefs, is often the easy victim of the first sophist he meets when at last he faces the indifferent or hostile world, so the American brought up in a blind and loyal acceptance of American institutions as self-evidently the best is not immune from sudden doubt when he meets astute disbelievers.

The number of Americans exposed to this test of faith is small and, while it is desirable that the American soldier should have a better instructed and more living faith, the chief danger does not lie in the imperfect morale of the armed forces. It is in the average American's picture of the outside world and in his inadequate judgment of what he can expect of the outside world and of his own government that the danger of disillusionment or of irrelevant reaction lies—and the consequent danger of losing the competitive game that, as an American citizen, he must play or have his government play for him.

What are the first of these illusions that color the American mind and make the task of the American government more difficult? The first is what I propose to call the political fallacy of mere imitation. There is naturally in the American mind an underestimate of the difficulty of transplanting political institutions and an excessive belief in the virtue of names and of formally similar political institutions.

There are good historical reasons for this easy belief in the virtue and universal exchangeability of worlds. As Lord

Acton pointed out, the American Revolution laid down, as the basis of government, principles asserted to be of universal application. It created institutions that professed to owe their authority to universal principles and to be the creation of that historical generation. Alone among the great nations of the world the United States has an official birthday and an official birth certificate. Alone among the great nations of the world it dates solemn documents by the year of its independence. No doubt to a good Soviet citizen the greatest event in the history of the world is the October Revolution. But Russia existed before the Russian Soviet Republic. Leningrad is not, like Washington, the creation of the new state. Possibly Canadians feel about Dominion Day as Americans feel about the Fourth of July (I doubt it). But Canada existed as a legal entity and as a historical fact before 1867. Australians do not even pretend to celebrate the establishment of the Commonwealth as a great national holiday. July 14 is an ambiguous festival for many Frenchmen and the Queen's birthday is imperfectly observed in England.

His popular tradition, his schooling, his memories of childhood, and the whole pressure of his historical environment make the American take easily to the view that a government, a new nation "conceived in liberty," can easily be set up by an effort of will and that the organizing of a government after that effort of will is a matter of good sense and good faith, both being most manifestly displayed in imitating the American way. The American, then, has in recent years been shocked both by the reluctance of many new nations to imitate the first modern, free nation and by the ambiguous result of such imitation as there has been.

Thus (and I think this the most conspicuous example of his misunderstanding) the American associates democracy and freedom. He thinks that a government should base its authority on nothing less than the consent of the majority (the practically unanimous consent of the people is needed for the *establishment* of a truly legitimate government) and that government so established should always be subject to legal dismissal, should not be thought to have an unlimited power of action, and should have as its final cause, as the aim that justifies its existence, individual freedom and responsibility. Its product is free men, not some vague generalized state called "national freedom."

Naturally enough, the American thinks that the best way to achieve this desirable end is to imitate the American way of attaining it. Has not history shown in the United States, by American methods, how government best promoted freedom, prosperity, political equality, equality of opportunity, and produced such obviously beneficial results as the American standard of living and the abundance that has permitted the American generosity to which, he rightly feels, the world owes so much? He is shocked, then, to discover that for the new nations coming to birth, to which he has often acted as both midwife and fairy godmother, the road to the best life does not seem so open, so easy, so inevitably taking an American form. The American's vision of his own history blinds him to its unique character.

The word "revolution," like "democracy" and like "freedom," is ambiguous. I would not for a moment deny that the American Revolution in its principles, largely in its practice, and in its results was truly revolutionary. But it was a revolution of a special kind, taking place in a society of a very special kind. The contrast is not only with the new nations of Asia and Africa but with the new nations that arose from the ruins of the Spanish Empire. There are many reasons why their history has been so unlike that of the United States, but one obvious reason is the very different historical environment in which the new nations of Spanish America (and the new nation of Brazil) came into being. Their separation from the mother country involved the creation of a complete set of new political institutions, largely copied in form from those of the United States. But the new nation that came to birth in 1776 (I apologize to any unreconstructed Confederates) inherited a great part of its institutions from the old order and, what was equally important, inherited a great part of its political and social spirit from the old order. It inherited legal and political institutions that were fairly easily transformed into postcolonial institutions. Representative government (no doubt in very imperfect forms) and legal institutions that assumed representative government, these were serious assets. So was the habit of relying on legal precedent, the tradition of the charters, of the Mayflower Compact, of the New England town meeting. So was the necessity of toleration rather than the theory of toleration. Because all creeds were represented in the colonies, from Catholics to Quakers, because there were colleges of all denominations, like Harvard and Rutgers, because the English government had not the means even if it had the will to impose as much uniformity and discrimination as it did at home, the new nation set out with a mature political tradition that not only treasured freedom but gave a concrete institutional and legal meaning to it. I am not so naïve as not to know that other forces were and are at work in American life, forces making for uniformity, for tyranny, for discrimination. I have not read Tocqueville or lived in the America of the Ku-Klux Klan (not to speak of later aberrations) for nothing. But the tradition of tolerated, even of admired, dissent is as deep as the tradition of enforced conformity, the institutions that protect the minorities, the unpopular individual, that insist on the freeman as the aim of political society have proved, in the long run, always victorious even if the battle has to be fought over and over again.

The American, contemplating the liberation of the old colonial territories of Britain, the Netherlands, France, sees them too easily in terms of his own fortunate and unique experience. I would not assert that nothing was lost in the violent separation from the British crown. (The history of Canada could suggest some of the things that were lost.) But most that was valuable in the colonial experience was saved and was used.

The history of the new nations of today is very different. For one thing, the American colonists had only recently ceased considering themselves Englishmen or, at any rate, contented British subjects. They did not and could not see in their past subjection to imperial authority the root of all evil and in their previous status an intolerable humiliation. They saw a stage that they had outgrown but one no more to be disowned than childhood is to be disowned in manhood.

To think of this situation as casting much light on the problems of a nation suffering from the humiliation of rule by an obviously foreign power, naturally less willing to ask itself what accounted for the fact of that rule than to attribute nearly all the weaknesses of the human situation to foreign "imperialism," is to be naïve. And to expect the new nations to attain, simply by a decision of the will and some willingness to get down to work, the state of the colonies in 1776, much less the state of the United States in 1959, is to be dangerously naïve. It leads to two errors, each to be deplored. It leads to an optimistic evasion of the awkward truth that probably few nations outside Europe today can hope by *any* means to attain anything like the American standard of well-being; consequently it leads to an underestimate of how much help the new nations need and how desperate their condition often is. And, second, from an overestimate of the ease with which "freedom" will result in well-being it is easy to slip into a too-facile despair. Because a new nation—in India, in Java—does not repeat visibly and easily the happy history of the United States it is too often written off as beyond or beneath help and its real achievements (and India at least has some remarkable achievements) are neglected because they are not on the American pattern or do not give all the results that, it is innocently assumed, an imitation of American methods would make possible.

There is another consequence of this misjudging of the situation of the new nations, of the nations coming to birth, or of the nations of Latin America belatedly entering the modern industrial world. The element of time is forgotten. All these nations are engaged in a race against time. It may be a race (as in India and perhaps in part of Latin America) against a galloping birth rate, for what matters is not the "net reproduction rate" but the pressure of that rate upon resources. And in my opinion at least equally important is the race against expectation. One of the great revolutionary forces at work in the world today is the universal prevalence of the idea that human life *can* be better, that hunger and premature death are not inevitable, that mankind is far more master of its fate than, in most societies for thousands of years, anybody had thought possible. The old contentment of habit is over; the cake of custom is broken. Amelioration of the human condition is known to be possible and is taken as a natural right. "The pursuit of happiness" is world-wide and urgent.

In that pursuit it is natural that other aims should suffer. Notably the Western, above all the American, idea of freedom suffers. The starving man, racked by endemic disease, conscious that elsewhere life is better but either with no idea of how it can be better for him or with naïve political ideas of how it can be made better, will naturally put what are first things first—for him. And he may not be morally or practically wrong if he thinks that many of the ways in which America has attained her well-being are beyond his means. I do not mean beyond the material resources of the new nations, although that is a sad truth about many of them. (What a pity that oil and deserts seem to go together!) I mean rather that the elaborate and social structure of

America, of which politics are only a part and an expression (though a most important part and expression), is for historical reasons not simply exportable to countries with an inheritance of the caste system, of illiteracy, of absolute rule from above, and with a very inadequate middle class and no real business class at all.

I shall have to speak of these aspects of American society later and have not the time nor would it be proper for me to dwell on the theme here. But, given the time pressure, to remake the world on an American model is a vain dream if the Americans insist on the exact imitation of every detail of their social and political institutions.

It will be a tragic error if you Americans do not allow enough for the deceptive flexibility with which your Communist rivals approach the task of seducing the most energetic, public-spirited, and competent of the youth of these nations with *their* recipe for a speedy escape from the morass of tradition, that is, the imposition of the new, technological way of life in the name of a "liberating" doctrine on societies too backward (so the argument runs) to breed an informed demand for the necessary means to the universally accepted end.

Since the United States is incapable of entering into this field of authoritarian transformation—debarred by its own doctrines, by its own healthy skepticism, by its own disagreements as to what is the good life—it can win and keep friends only by showing that the American system works at home and that it is capable not of being exported but of being a source of disinterested, intelligent, and timely aid to peoples deeply suspicious of the motives of all outsiders and unwilling to admit that some, at any rate, of their troubles come from internal and curable defects. But it is a hundred times more valuable for a new nation (or an old nation) to learn that sad truth about itself from its own experience than to be told it by even the most good-tempered and well-meaning outsiders who, having made their own way in the world, cannot see why in a much more crowded, much more hurried, much more threatened world their example cannot be easily copied.

The world may forgive American wealth; it may even be willing to admit that it is mainly earned by American industry and capacity, but it will not willingly listen to sermons on the easy way out of poverty from a nation that at no time in its fortunate history has known the dire straits that have been for most of the human race the common and necessary lot.

What this involves for the American political system is, I hope, obvious. The problem is not to export in bulk the American way of running the state and the economy; it is to run it visibly well in America. Even if the outside world will not deliberately imitate the American way, even if it cannot imitate the American way, it will be impressed or repelled by the success or the failure of the American way of doing America's business at home. And, as I must be permitted to remind you, the superiority of American methods is so far from being taken for granted that in a great part of the world there is a bias against believing that the Americans can manage even their own affairs at home. Unjustly but not totally unnaturally, jealousy, ignorance, and dogmatism ensure that a great many American attempts to present the American way of doing things start with two strikes on them. " 'Tis true, 'tis pity; and pity 'tis 'tis true."

How does the American political system look from the outside, as seen by a friendly but critical observer like myself? I have begun by insisting on the success of the American experiment and by accepting and approving of the American loyalty to it. But I have also suggested that this very loyalty often blinds the American to some of the limitations of that success, and he takes for granted alike merits and defects. He may not be totally unwise in doing this. He may think and be right in thinking that some defects are the necessary price of some merits. Thus nothing is easier than to show up the absurdity of the American party system, the near identity of the party programs, the irrelevance of many of the historical appeals, the casual and merely historical nature of party allegiance over a great part of the country. Demands for a "responsible party system" come often enough from my own profession, that of the political scientists of America. Again and again the voter is commiserated with on the situation in which he finds himself. He is often enough in an area where only one party can win and where party predominance is secured by memories of the Civil War or, if you like, of the War Between the States. He is reminded of how little it often means that one party wins a national election, how fictitious is party unity, how empty party discipline. Even if over this vast country an identifiable tide of public feeling can be observed, it usually trickles out (so we are told) in the shallows and miseries of the division of powers, of the control of Congress by committee chairmen, of the open conspiracy of the veteran leaders on both sides of the aisles to keep change down to a minimum.

Can we wonder, we are asked, that the American so often refuses to vote and thus shames American democracy before the more civically virtuous British and French, not to speak of the practically unanimous and disciplined voters of the "people's democracies"? All these charges are true; but this is another matter to which I shall return, to assess their importance and offset them against some uncovenanted benefits.

For long enough enlightened citizens and progressive lawyers have assailed the unique American institution of judicial review which guaranteed not the government of the people, by the people, for the people, but the government of the people by lawyers for their opulent clients. What could be more absurd, on paper, than a system that makes possible the return of a president of one party and a Congress of another? When this happened for the first time after World War II in circumstances certainly no more dangerous than those which now confront us, Senator Fulbright suggested that the President of his own party, Mr. Truman, should resign. Mr. Truman naturally did not see things that way and had his revenge on Senator Fulbright (and on millions of other people including me) in 1948. But since then we have had three more Congresses with this division of powers and the worst disasters have not befallen the United States or the cause for which it stands. Mr. Truman got from a Republican Congress the means of the Marshall Plan and Mr. Eisenhower has not visibly suffered much from purely partisan opposition.

It is argued that these obsolete political institutions diminish interest in politics, that the American citizen seems to be a bad or an indifferent citizen because federal politics and, still more, state politics are not dramatic; the distance between voting and any visible result of voting is too remote and hazardous for it to be reasonable to expect the average man to turn from his own private business to the affairs of state with any eagerness or competence.

I could multiply the complaints, all of them formally cogent and justified; I could add to them. There is the problem of the organs of public opinion, the mass media, the role of advertising—a whole series of problems on which I shall have something to say later. What I shall try to do here is not to deny the validity of the complaints but rather to show another side of the medal and suggest that the outside world need not take the American political situation as tragically as many Americans do.

The irrationality of the party system, for instance, may be the necessary price paid for the unity of so vast and diverse a country. Would a rationalized party system necessarily be a two-party system and how would national unity stand up under the strain of a multiparty system? What is the basis of a rational party system to be? Can it simply be a class system, of the haves against the have-nots? Is foreign policy the natural and decisive dividing line, as Professor C. Wright Mills has recently suggested, and do Americans want or can the United States—or the free world—afford a party system devoted to an endless debate over foreign policy that might well suit the purposes of the Soviet Union better than the safety or needs of the American people?

The division of powers to which so much critical attention is directed may no longer be defensible on eighteenth-century grounds. Too much history has altered the balance of power within the American constitutional system for the old fears of congressional aggression to seem very real. But the genius of the American system has produced in the presidency a solution to a problem that harasses the new nations—and some of the older ones. It is surely worth noting that the drift of constitutional practice is toward the presidential rather than the parliamentary system, that a crude version of the American system seems more relevant to the needs of the new nations than the more complicated British parliamentary system, which calls for so many subtle understandings that it can be even less exported (outside the Commonwealth at least) than can the presidential system.

In any case, there can be no doubt that for the outside world it is the presidency that counts; effective leadership must come from the White House and, ex officio, the President of the United States is leader of the free world. The history of the presidency suggests that Woodrow Wilson was right, that the office is as big as the man who fills it, and to have an office with that capacity for expansion, that power of evoking respect—I might say reverence—inside the United States and something like understanding outside it is an achievement of which the framers of the Constitution have reason to be proud. Naturally no one can provide for succession of adequate presidents, but the office is there if the man can be found. In how many lands is the legal opportunity for adequate leadership present? In how many lands have there not been breakdowns in leadership at least as dangerous as any that can be found in recent American leadership? Certainly not in Britain!

This is not to say that the American political system has not some built-in defects that are expensive and dangerous in our troubled age. There is, for instance, the neglected limitation on the weight of the House of Representatives caused by the locality rule. This means that in many sections of the Union able men who have the misfortune to belong to the wrong party are debarred from a congressional career. This means, in turn, that the House of Representatives and even the Senate suffer from the known fact that they do not necessarily contain the ablest politicians or men who would willingly make politics their career, but simply the most successful local politicians of districts and states, some of the districts being barely in the modern world and some of the states being anomalies hard to justify today.

Less defensible is the seniority rule. I do not think it is true that a federal system necessarily imposes a locality rule. Canada is there to prove the contrary. But the Constitution does impose some kind of locality rule and the reverence that makes the American hesitate to tamper with the sacred text is almost always justified. But there can be no such defense of the seniority rule. That tradition, in its most rigorous form not very old, puts power not necessarily into wrong but often into irrelevant hands, hands that by definition become too old yet cannot be pried loose from, at any rate, negative authority and hands that by definition do not represent the more flexible, less party-bound, more modern and open-minded parts of the country. The result of the locality rule plus the seniority rule is to give to much of the public business of the House, and even of the Senate, a parish pump air that accounts for the comparative indifference with which the American public regards its national politicians and the odd impression they sometimes make on the outside world.

I do not assert that a different organization of Congress would necessarily alter the tariff policy or the farm policy of Congress, but it might make it easier for the view to be expressed and even listened to that the allies of the United States and the uncommitted neutrals are involved—however wrong it may seem to the old 100 per cent American—even in strictly local decisions to pile up farm surpluses, to limit importations of oil or metals, or to save the United States from the dangers of English electrical machinery.

Yet I cannot think that the United States is prevented from having an effective foreign policy or from giving a lead based on generosity as well as power because of these defects in the parliamentary system. No more do I think that miraculous results would follow from the only constitutional change that I *do* advocate, the extension of the term of the House of Representatives to four years. I think the arguments against this change are merely traditional, that the arguments for it are serious; but even if I were an American citizen I might not campaign for the change with any great fervor on the principle of letting fairly well enough alone.

It is hardly necessary today to point out that the old charges against the Supreme Court have been replaced by new ones. It is as an enemy of the proper distribution of powers between Union and states that the Court is attacked. It is as a usurper of power in the interests not of big business but of a doctrinaire sociology that the Court is treated as a long arm of the Kremlin. Yet the Court's decision in the segregation cases did not create the crisis; it merely underlined the irony of the race problem in a nation "dedicated to the proposition that all men are created equal."

Even the oldest traditions of the United States show signs of adaptation to the times. When there are Republican congressmen in the South and a 100 per cent Democratic delegation from Vermont in the House, the old sneers about the merely traditional character of American politics lose much of their force.

The problem of American democracy today is only in a minor degree one of mechanics, although mechanics are something. It is a question of the spirit. Can the American people helpfully adjust themselves to a world that regards them with envy and hostility as well as with admiration and a certain amount of critical trust? Can the American people accept the limitations on their power of action and power of leadership? Can they accept less, much less than their own way, if they can help to steer the old world entering the new world of industry and well-being with so much pain, difficulty, error and folly? Can the American people both lead and support their politicians when remembering that great responsibilities and little minds go ill together—if I may alter Burke's dictum?

I don't know the answers. I only have a faith that if the American people take the advice of Lincoln and find out where they are and where, unless they are bold, generous and open-minded, they are destined to go—to hell in the modern equivalent of a handcart—they will with their prodigious energy and their deep if sometimes clouded sense of human responsibility justify their own democratic faith and works in a world that would rather be aided than kicked around and improved for its own good by countries and parties that know—and say they know—what that good is. Modesty has never been accounted an American virtue, but it may be the best American card today. In the unwonted sense of bewilderment and humility that has befallen the American people in the past year or two there is a chance that this new virtue added to the old will restore to the American people that leadership that the world deeply wants, the leadership of a people that is willing to learn as well as to teach, that will yet suffer fools gladly and see fools at home as well as abroad.

3

The Character of American Life

I am only too conscious of the boldness, the absurdity, of undertaking to say anything of interest or even of minimal good sense on so vast a topic as the character of American life. Despite the boldness of my title, I am more timid or more sensible than may appear and what I propose is to attempt something bold enough in itself and yet more practicable than the vast adventure which my title might suggest.

I shall begin by saying that there are vast areas of American life that I shall ignore. Most of what may be called political economy I shall slip away from. I have no doubt that the economic problems of the farmer are deeply important and reveal something of the character of American life, but I shall do no more than bow at the problem, be silent on the solution, and deal with the farmer only as part of the rapidly changing panorama of American society. There is the role of American women; I shall not ignore it entirely, but again there are many problems concerned with her status, her social and economic role that I shall ignore, both from timidity and from wisdom. For example, I shall not develop my belief that the American woman is to some extent a victim of a confidence trick played by the American man—who is much smarter than the American woman realizes and gives to her more the appearance than the reality of power and equality. The vast fields covered by "education" and "culture" I shall deal with separately and, without apology, ignore here.

I shall try to say something positive, but I shall try to pick on *some* salient marks of American society, of American life, both for their intrinsic interest and for their relevance to my basic theme—the competitive strength of the United States in the dangerous world in which it now has to live. That is to say, I shall make some parallels with European society, stressing resemblances as well as differences. And I shall try to weigh some features of American life, if not quite like an observer from outer space at least with the comparative objectivity of a foreigner.

Comparative objectivity, for it would be idle to pretend that I come here as a stranger or a neutral. If I may be permitted some autobiography, I first came to the United States nearly thirty-four years ago when I had just left Oxford, having created some scandal there by insisting on going to America to study the scarcely respectable subject of American history. I have visited America nearly every year since; I even managed to make three visits during the war, and I have sometimes made more than one visit in a year. Altogether I have spent six or seven years in this country and its study has been my chief academic and literary activity since I first came here, an innocent pilgrim, in the golden day of Calvin Coolidge. I come not really as a neutral but as a most friendly observer who has tried hard to understand this country and to pass on what knowledge he has acquired to his often moderately receptive countrymen. Whatever I do, however hard I try to be the stern impartial critic, friendliness and optimism will keep creeping in.

Catholics talk of the "marks" of the Church and I should like to begin by describing some of the marks of American society as I see them. First I shall follow in the footsteps of my great predecessor, Alexis de Tocqueville, and stress the mark of equality. No one not blinded by prejudice, no one knowing Britain or France or Germany, can fail to be struck by the fact that "equality" is as much a distinguishing mark of American society as it was one hundred thirty years ago when Tocqueville made his famous journey.

True, there are apparent differences. There are far more rich people today than there were then; there are many more millions of Americans who can be classified as part of "le peuple," as Tocqueville's countrymen put it then and now. Economic inequality is more visible now than it was then. Then, if we believe Tocqueville, the rich rather concealed their wealth and if they enjoyed it they enjoyed it in secret. They played it down if they wished to enter politics and an ostentatious display of democratic tastes was called for in candidates for public office. It would be wrong today to deny that candidates profess an enthusiasm that may be genuine for hot dogs and blintzes, for baseball and basketball. But few doubted in 1958 that Governor Harriman or Nelson Rockefeller normally lived on rather more sophisticated diet than what may be called electoral nutriment or that, if they had democratic tastes, they also had tastes whose gratification required very large incomes. There is no cheap, democratic way of collecting French Impressionists, no really democratic way of playing polo; and it is notorious that ex-Governor Harriman and Governor Rockefeller are more than comfortably off and that other governors, many senators, and even a few lesser public figures are at least comfortably off. It may not help them politically (I refuse to speculate) but it does not visibly hurt them. The American voter has got used to economic inequality and no longer resents it in itself. Nor does he resent even the most outrageous display of conspicuous consumption by what is called, I believe, "café society," except possibly when he is paying his modest income tax and wondering what it is like to have a really fat expense account. The popular idols of the screen, the stage, and TV are expected to show appreciation of their good fortune by garish display, and even in contemplating the Texas oil millionaire who can't have a swimming pool because every time he builds one he strikes oil the American is inclined to say "nice work if you can get it" rather than "Workers of the world, unite."

My examples of an American attitude have not been chosen quite at random or to provoke easy laughter. Behind them lies an American attitude that Tocqueville did not stress, although I find it hard to believe that it was not visible in his time and it is certainly very visible and worth noting in our time. The United States is a country in which simple jealousy plays a comparatively innocuous and unimportant role in political and social life. Note I do not say in private life. I have read too many powerful novels, too many reports of murder trials when all went black and there on the floor was a dead husband or wife, not to know that Americans are subject to the human if ignoble emotion of jealousy just like other people. But if Americans can endure or even accept with ease a great deal of economic and social inequality in public life, in economic life, in sport and diversion, it is in great part because of the absence of jealousy in the American attitude.

No one who has moved around in England, France or Germany can doubt that in all these countries jealous, resentful envy is an important source of political animus and of national disunion and weakness. Why is America different?

I shall advance a thesis that is not very novel and not very profound, but has, I think, the advantage of making this important difference appear not simply as an inexplicable difference or even as a proof of American stupidity and gullibility. (If the American common man knew his business as a common man he would be jealous. So many a European intellectual argues—though perhaps not quite in those words.)

The American political and economic environment has been from the beginning unkind to pretensions that did not have some apparent relation to achievement either in the present or in the recent and what may be called the "usable" past. It is a commonplace of American historiography that all attempts to export feudalism failed. The European entrepreneur who wanted to turn his assets into a political and social superiority that he could leave to his family was making a mistake if he took his capital to British North America. For various reasons that I can do no more than allude to it proved impossible to set up a hereditary landowning or office-owning class to which admission would be slow, irregular, and not important enough in numbers to flood the existing class structure in each generation to a degree that would destroy its exclusiveness.

I hasten to say that I am not under the illusion that there are no social fences in America, no social barriers that are hard to pass, no cult of exclusiveness. Indeed it could be said that some American social groups are more exclusive than their European counterparts, less willing to admit the promoting power of money. I have lived in Boston and visited Philadelphia!

But even in their great days, the Back Bay and the Main Line were not accepted as their English or French and, still more, German equivalents were, as part of the nature of things. They were picturesque anomalies with, I suspect, more power to bruise than to hurt seriously and less power to give pleasure and comfort than the aspiring climbers hoped. What was and is the use of being admitted to an exclusive society if the vast majority of those excluded don't really care or, what is worse, don't really know that they are being excluded?

The very emphasis on barriers, on clubs, on fraternities,

on exclusive schools and pools reveals a social order in which equality is constantly intruding, in which it takes a lot of money and energy and, I should suggest, a high degree of humorlessness, to get men and women to take the trouble to exclude and to include on any grounds but those of social fitness and utility and personal attraction. An English student from Oxford or Cambridge introduced to the full rigors of the secret society system at Yale is astounded and amused or horrified, according to temperament and political bias. But if he is a good observer and remembers Oxford or Cambridge when he is at Yale he will, I think, be forced to conclude that Yale, for all the mystery of Bones, is more democratic than either Oxford or Cambridge, where the barriers are less visible, less stressed but far more difficult to surmount and far more wounding to fail to surmount. I have deliberately chosen an academic example, partly because I know both Oxford and Cambridge well and have seen something of Yale, but partly because it is in the American school system, in its widest sense, that equality and inequality fight a perpetual battle which inequality always loses.

Elsewhere I shall suggest that this is not always a good thing, but it is sufficient for the moment to note that economic inequality in America has, in the main, only economic consequences. As Scott Fitzgerald put it in his celebrated dialogue with Hemingway, "The rich are not like us." "Yes, they have more money," said Hemingway. I would be the last to deny that having more money is important; but having less money is even more important, for the poor suffer from their poverty more than the rich gain from their wealth. Yet in America merely having more money pays less in extra dividends, less in bought servility, less in reverence or its opposite, envious rancor, than it does in any other country known to me.

Because it is assumed (often wrongly) that wealth represents past or present useful service to the economy or, what the average man appreciates quite as much, the democracy of more luck—more luck in striking an oil well, more luck in answering in the dear dead days the $64,000 question—the American takes inequalities in his stride. He may be a victim of an illusion. He probably exaggerates, if not for himself, then for his children their chances of promotion in the economic and social scale. He may neglect the power of the power elite in a naïve way. He may even think that his political rights give him in the mass some control over the power elite and that money and the control of the economy are not everything (in my opinion he is right in so thinking), but here we are concerned not with his intelligence, his power of judgment *sub specie orbis*. A man who feels happy is happy; a man who is contented, by and large, has in that attitude a source of happiness that is not to be neglected or despised. In the pursuit of happiness the race may be to the swift and the handicapping not quite just, but it is an asset for a country that the race is believed to be so open that nearly everybody wants to run in it.

This attractiveness of the race accounts for the good temper with which, in general, its results are accepted as beneficial, which is a great social asset. If the contentment of the American were a passive contentment, if it were contentment not with the general system but with his particular place in it, as has often been the meaning of contentment in torpid, tradition-ridden societies, then much could be said for stirring up discontent, divine or simply human. But I think it can hardly be denied that one source of American wealth has been the belief in the rewards of economic virtue and the adequate correspondence of that belief with the facts.

Turning for a moment to the outside world, it must be stressed that the role of this competitive spirit, this American theory of the economic game, is not fully understood anywhere else and over a great part of the world is not understood at all. Contemplating the American economic miracle, the European and still more the Asian or the African is not as a rule willing to allow for the role of the businessman or to accept the fact that to get his particular type of social usefulness he must be willing to ignore formal economic equality or the pretense of it, must be willing to accept in their role as entrepreneurs some very rough diamonds and perhaps some persons who are not even semi-precious stones. The European, the Asian, the African, in a descending order of comprehension, finds it hard to believe that the highest virtues and the highest talents can possibly be observed in a man who devotes the greater part of his life to the accumulation of wealth.

But one will rightly protest, the American businessman as a type does not devote himself to the accumulation of wealth as such; he devotes himself to the production of wealth and his share in it, handsome as it may be, is only a legitimate price for what he gives society in his pursuit of the satisfactions of the business life. This I believe to be true. But at the risk of seeming to lay down general laws that cannot be proved I shall assert that this acceptance of the business life as one worthy of calling out all the powers of a really able man, giving him the satisfactions of a really worthy lifework, may not be solely American but it is peculiarly American. And it is one of the reasons why America is so wealthy and so comparatively free from the crippling social barriers and social resentments of Europe.

Maurice Zinkin has argued that what India needs is more good businessmen and more respect for good businessmen. I believe this is true also of Britain and even of that businessman's paradise, Western Germany. To be epigrammatic at the risk of seeming foolish I should say that outside the United States more respect for business achievement is needed and inside the United States one should, without losing one's natural respect for the businessman for what he does well, be more willing to accept the possibility that there are things well worth doing that businessmen cannot do and that cannot be done in a "businesslike way."

Given the American experience, where most successful social enterprises have been run by businessmen for businessmen (and for the economy in general as well), it is natural that this experience should be extended to the outside world. But, in the first place, it is too simple a view of American history to see the growth of the American economy as taking place without political direction, without the state's playing more than a minor or a positively nefarious role. The American businessman owes both the existence of his opportunities and the character of his opportunities to the success of the United States as a body politic. The existence of the Union was necessary in order to create the American market and so was its maintenance. Thus Madison and Hamilton, Lincoln and Grant—none of them, not even Hamilton, a business type—are among the most potent makers of the American market and so of the American economy in which the American businessman has flourished.

I shall dogmatically assert that a Lincoln is not only a more interesting but a much more important figure than a Ford or a Rockefeller. Someone would have invented the equivalent of the Model T or the Standard Oil Company. But Lincolns are scarcer and in 1861 the United States could not have afforded to wait until the turn of the wheel brought up an equivalent of Lincoln and put him into the White House. This is the first important modification of the exalted picture I have honestly painted of the role and the utility of the American businessman. He has played so useful a role and his role has been so handsomely rewarded in cash and credit that he has naturally been tempted to exalt himself even above his merits, which are great, and by implication to denigrate other groups whose essential services to the American experiment have been as great but not so well rewarded as those of the businessman.

The businessman has as a rule taken an ironical view of the politician. He has seen him as a parasite, as a tool, sometimes as a demagogic nuisance who has to be fought or bought off or suffered not in silence but in noisy wrath. He has contrasted the things that business does (and usually does well) with the things the political organizations have done—at every level, city, county, state, nation—and has stressed the things that these political units have done badly—and there are many of them. He has tended to forget that not all businesses have been well run; the bankruptcy courts show that.

The history of American railroads is not an argument for leaving all to the businessman and if some of the energetic men who made great fortunes out of the railroads were national benefactors some were morally on the level of Jesse James and charged a high price for their services, a high price in money and a higher price in damage to the social and political fabric. I am aware that things have changed, that the days of the robber barons are over or almost over (it is harder to be a robber baron than it used to be; there are more policemen of various kinds). But even if we believe all that business tells us about itself—and I don't believe quite all of it—we have to remember that in many parts of the world the robber barons are still with us and are not, even in the kindest and most generous eyes, as much builders as were some of the most rapacious of the leaders and makers and exploiters of the American economy of the second half of the nineteenth century.

The American businessman, looking abroad and conscious of the services he renders (and charges quite highly for), is liable to ignore important facts about the outside world, facts that alter the picture he paints for himself and imposes on the American government, facts that demand a toleration of "unbusinesslike" methods that shocks the doctrinaires of "free enterprise." If the United States is going to have an economic foreign policy it will have to deal with societies in which there is no business class or a disastrously rapacious and incompetent business class and in which the only substitute for the absent competent businessman is the state. And the state may be the only competent manager of large-scale enterprise that the country in question either has or can hope to have in the not-unlimited time of competition with the rival Soviet system. This is, I think, the case in India and will continue to be the case in the critical years in which the fate of India—and more than the fate of India—will be decided.

Thus the exaltation of the businessman in the United States, the belief that the standards of the American business economy are easily exported and that there is something sinful in not admitting this fact, is a great handicap to the government of the United States in its economic foreign policy. It may be necessary to strengthen "socialist" economies, to accept irritating political controls, to tolerate what are, objectively, absurdly wasteful ways of doing things simply because the world happens to be like that and most foreign societies have no choice: they have no more right to have an effective business class than they have to have an equivalent of Niagara Falls or of the Grand Canyon.

It is only partly a paradox to suggest that the American businessman (who sets the tone of a great deal of American life though perhaps not quite so much as he thinks and as his predecessors did) is too modest. He underestimates his own uniqueness. And when painful experience teaches him that the business methods of other societies are very different from and very inferior to his he is less prone to go up to the altar of the temple and thank God that he is not as other men than to think up ways of converting the inferior European or Asian or African model into a 100 per cent imitation of the 100 per cent American businessman.

This generous ambition is a foolish one. Though the American businessman is less conscious than he should be of his unique character, he is more conscious than he should be of his unique role in making the American way of life that business has so deeply and, on the whole, so beneficially marked. For the American economy is only a part of the American way of life; the American businessman is only one of the makers of the American economy. I have already alluded to the role of the politician in making and preserving the Union. But I would rank as equally important the role of the politician in producing the illusion (which has, I hold, often been the reality) of a nonbusiness power that could protect the average man both in his interests and in his sentiments. The democratic way of life, American version, has been largely a matter of making—not final, not profound, not revolutionary—adjustments in the way in which the American economy was run, adjustments that for a great part of its formative period, made the necessary harshness of that economy tolerable and did not destroy the faith of the average man in the American way. For there is apparently no way in which an economy can make the take-off, to use Professor W. W. Rostow's admirable metaphor, that does not involve suffering, injustice, flagrantly unequal ways of paying the costs, and the destruction of old and comforting habits.

The histories of Britain and the United States, of the Soviet Union and Communist China alike tell this story. That the story as told in the United States has been one of a continuing faith in the American process is due, as much as to any other group, to the much-maligned politicians who, high as was their price, delivered the goods, the climate of opinion, of generosity, of admiration for achievement in which the American businessman has flourished. And to return to my first theme, the American businessman has been the chief but not the sole maker of the American economic way of life and deserves half the praise he gives himself; and this is, I suspect, about the amount of praise that the American non-businessman gives him in his friendly but rather skeptical fashion.

I have already dealt, though necessarily briefly, with the mechanics of the American political system and their relevance to the contemporary world of political competition. Now, dealing with the marks of American society, it is necessary to say something of the mark that the American politician represents. Earlier I spoke of the special service, the fundamental service that the politician has rendered in creating and preserving the Union and in creating the climate of opinion in which the businessman has been able to work with such success. I now want to describe briefly not only the achievement of the politician but his methods, the peculiar contribution he makes to the American way of doing things and the revelation of the character of American society that this political way provides.

I have alluded to the low ideological content of American party politics and have indicated my doubts as to whether the United States would gain by adopting rigorously doctrinaire systems of party differentiation and organization. Here I shall take it for granted that a political system which organizes democratic choice of persons and, very loosely, controls pressures from one group or another, serves a useful purpose and preserves a higher degree of human values than does the rival and in many ways efficacious system that we call communism. For communism, we must remember, is a *political* solution to the economic problem of the forced-draft progress of a backward agrarian society into the modern technological society. It is the political omnipotence of the Russian Communist party that accounts for Sputnik, as well as for the now-visible economic progress to the threshold of abundance that marks the Soviet Union.

The problem in a sense is the same everywhere. How is one to provide the necessary political authority without which the jump over to the more abundant life, to Professor Galbraith's affluent society, cannot be made? Within wide political controls, often intermittent in action, the American method has been to leave the specifically economic problems to a specifically economic class and to leave the organization of consent to this delegation of power and the tempering of its results to a specifically political class. The two classes, naturally, are never in a state of complete harmony or mutually supporting cooperation. There is almost always an imbalance and one can, I think, see two such imbalances in recent American history: in favor of politics under Presidents Roosevelt and Truman; in favor of business under President Eisenhower. Neither imbalance was necessarily wrong, at the time it occurred, and I ostentatiously refrain from asserting that either was necessarily right.

But, given this distribution of functions and this imbalance, what has been the peculiarly American character, the American mark of the American politician? It has not been true all the time that the American politician was not a doctrinaire. Jefferson was one of the most skilled, perhaps the most skilled, of American politicians but he was by temperament a doctrinaire. There was a basic unshakable bias in Lincoln, a bias in favor of human as against legal or property rights, a conviction that some institutions, however respectable by age, however plausible their claims as practical solutions, were wrong. But, like Jefferson, Lincoln was what is called a "practical politician." He worked, and knew he could only work, in the terms given by the American situation. Also, Lincoln was more self-critical than Jefferson and carefully distinguished between his public and his private duties and feelings. Neither was prepared to let the best be the enemy of the good. And in this sense of realities, in this readiness to separate the ideal from the immediately attainable, these two great Americans were representative and serviceable American politicians. They bear the American mark.

At the other end of the scale we have the moral equivalents of the "robber barons"—the city and state bosses. These, in their scientifically purest form, emptied politics of any trace of ideology that might have been found in it. Their allegiance to one party rather than the other—Democratic in New York, Republican in Philadelphia—was purely formal, purely traditional, and there is no known instance of their sacrificing their own interests and that of their organizations to the remote principles and needs of the national parties. Yet these odious figures played a useful, though expensive, part in the adjustment to the often painful and novel necessities of the American way of life of the millions of immigrants who provided the necessary labor force on whose blood, sweat, and tears the American economy was erected. The bosses may not notably have diminished the blood and sweat, but they did diminish the tears. They made the new society intelligible, tolerable, and gave it a human aspect, including in that aspect the very human attribute of erratic and all the more welcome favor.

That the bosses overcharged for their services is not to be doubted. They were brothers under the skin of the magnates who also overcharged but, like them, did in fact give much in return. And as in the parallel case of the business magnates, the greatest cost was not the cost in dollars, it was the cost in faith in the honest purpose of government, in the rational basis of society. If the average American still finds it difficult to take the purposes and practices of government seriously, or to understand European faith in the potentialities of government, that is part of the price paid for the rule of the bosses and for their utility (which I do not deny was real). And since there are a vast number of things that should be done, even in the United States, and that can be done only by state action, the price is still being paid. If this leads to the postponement of necessary action in the public sector, it may in the world we must live in have a very high price indeed.

But between the great national figures and the mere bosses there lay and still lies a useful and necessary class—the politicians, who are more than mere manipulators of consent though less than statesmen of long and adequately profound views. Because they are not doctrinaire, they are taken more seriously than if they set forth a system of coherent or allegedly coherent doctrines in the European fashion. That the American does not take intellectual coherence seriously enough is a proposition I shall advance in another context. But here I am concerned with a particular fact about American life, a mark of American life. That mark is the readiness of Americans to do things, to try experiments even though total consistency would debar them from trying the experiments, since they are often inconsistent with what is alleged to be the basic and unbreakable principle of American life.

For if principles will not break they will bend, and how adroit the American politician is in bending them! How many Americans appreciate enough the astonishing ingenuity of the primary system? When the late Senator Borah laid it down that, even if a candidate advocated the nationalization of the means of production, distribution and exchange, if he had won in a Republican primary he was a Republican, he turned with great boldness the flank of the unideological party system and made it possible for all doctrines to be advocated without any basic doctrines being called in question—or observed. Needless to say, there is an ugly side to this flexibility.

"You can have fascism in the United States. Only you must

call it antifascism." This alleged saying of the late Huey Long has about it an ominous ring of plausibility. Coming from a continent which has pursued consistency to the edge of suicide regarding a rival society that has not yet found a way of escaping from crippling and dangerous dogma, where it is still necessary in fact to find a harmony between the needs of the world of Sputnik and the H-bomb and the systematic intuitions of a man (Karl Marx) who died before the invention of the internal-combustion engine or of an economically effective dynamo, it is hard not to prefer the American way.

If there has been anything to worry about in the state of the American public mind in the past few years, it has been a tendency to react along doctrinaire lines, to be blinded by phrases, by slogans, by the erection of the slogans into systems of political action. Lincoln, Jefferson, Boss Tweed, and Senator Borah would have, in different ways, protested against this bad and new habit, and in our rapidly changing world to react to the doctrines and actions of the adversary merely on a plan of negation and contradiction laid down in advance is to be profoundly anti-American. But I firmly believe that the pragmatic genius of the American people will come to the rescue. So will the boredom of the American people with an attitude that does not pay off quickly and that calls for a degree of doctrinal rigidity which comes hard to the people who have taken the simple political structure of 1789 and have made of it a "more perfect union" than any Hamilton dreamed of.

Now to conclude. I have had to put on one side one of the most visible marks of the American genius, the proliferation of private organizations that strikes even a visitor from England with surprise and strikes a Frenchman or a German with far more surprise. These societies, service clubs, churches, organizations for all conceivable and some barely credible projects have been since Tocqueville's time a mark of American society. And they have, usually in a more respectable way, done much the same kind of service as the political machines. (I say usually, because a body like the Ku-Klux Klan is very American. Even the Mafia has taken on an American covering, and what could be less ideological than the higher direction of the Teamsters?)

The societies, secular as well as religious, have mediated between the vast, formal, often apparently inhuman claims of the "American way of life" and the harassed, intimidated, bewildered private citizen. They have also provided a channel for the zeal and energy of countless men and women whom the mere politics of the regular parties repelled or bored. To keep so much zeal from going sour is no small contribution to the commonwealth! And in the endless combinations and permutations of American societal life, the American is made to feel and act as a social and not as a merely economic or political animal. His total role in life has been enriched, even by intrinsically foolish activities.

Even the busybody is better than the type that the Greeks called "the idiot," the citizen who had no interest in the well-being of the commonwealth. To be a member of a society is as much the mark of the American as any I can think of. I can only note the fact and promise to deal with one or two aspects of it at another time.

But as I have expounded my, on the whole, optimistic view of the marks of American society I have been conscious of some natural skepticism: "Hasn't he read Riesman?" "Hasn't he read *The Organization Man?*" "Doesn't he know that the young today eschew the life of action and its risks and seek, in the womb of Big Business or Big Government, the security that they crave? What is the use of stressing the virtues and even the vices of traditional American polity when it is being changed visibly and at high speed under one's eyes?"

I have read both Mr. Riesman and Mr. Whyte; I have observed some of these phenomena for myself. I think that American society and, notably, American education require a great deal of rethinking in theory and in practice. I am aware that the high degree of mutual toleration that marks the class structure of contemporary America is, for some, simply a proof that the American people can be bought off by a share in the more abundant material life, that this toleration may not survive a serious falling off in economic well-being and that, as has been asserted, it is paid for very highly by the universal acceptance of a gadget-and-gimmick civilization. Socrates thought the unexamined life not worth living but the unexamined life is the American life of the current American ideal—if it can be dignified by such a noble name.

So runs the argument of the devil's advocate. I do not deny its plausibility or its important element of truth. But the "organization man" is not the only type of American nor even the only type of American businessman and he is not, as commonly pretended, the whole man of the organization chart. The organization ideal takes less out of a man and uses up less of the whole man than did the simple ferocious life of the businessman in pursuit of "the bitch goddess, Success" a generation ago. And the results of this loss of the full measure of devotion are, on the whole, good.

The United States is now affluent enough, if not to afford all that Professor Galbraith wants, at least to afford far more lazinesss and consequent opportunity for reflection than any past American generation has known. There may be a falling off in economic drive and productivity, but the competition to which I constantly recur is not only in material well-being but in real or alleged goods of the spirit, of what we loosely call culture. "Things are in the saddle, and ride mankind" was written a century ago. Was Emerson describing his age or prophesying ours? I think he was doing both, and one cure for some current pessimism is to look back at the plausible descriptions and predictions of doom that previous generations have listened to, with half an ear cocked and half a complete dose of faith in the prophets. I have no belief that American productive capacity and genius is in for any serious decline. My fears are of the direction that may be given to that capacity and genius.

If American society preserves, in necessarily modified forms, the marks that I have sought to identify, it will survive its ordeal. I think it can do now without bosses. Business will never again have and never again should have its old immunity from criticism and control. The national government will never be "cut down to size" in face of the political power of the Soviet Union and Communist China. The day (I am ready to say, alas!) is to the strong, the united, the politically dominated. But American society has immense historical as well as physical resources. If it can assess those assets correctly and take corrective action it will hold its own in the battle that is a battle for mankind's hopes as well as its fears.

If America can hold her own can she fail, in a not-limitlessly remote future, to win? For the "new man the American" represents not only a unique historical experience but an intrinsically attractive type of human possibility. If you (and we in Western Europe are included in that "you") can survive the immediate and terrible crisis that faces all of us, we shall find much working for us in men's minds and hearts. If we and you deserve leadership, it will be offered to us. And one of the ways that we can deserve it is for each of the countries of the Western alliance to hold to that which is good in its own traditions. If Americans do that, intelligently, the battle is more than half won and a great part of that half is, to be sure, in our own hearts, that we believe in and trust our way of dealing with the human situation. So far we have no need to fear comparison or competition.

4

American Education

I have already indicated one or two of the "marks" of American society and in so doing I have, until now, ignored what is certainly, as seen from the outside, one of its most conspicuous marks: its belief in education. No people in history (at any rate, no people known to me) have had a greater, I might say uncritical, belief in education than the Americans. Some peoples—the Germans and the Scots, and in more modern times the Russians—have had, perhaps, an equal belief in education, but I am not quite certain that this is so. The American is a man or woman who believes that most problems in life, perhaps all problems in life, can be dealt with by instruction before the problem arises. This is an exaggeration, but only a slight exaggeration.

Of course, not all Americans at all times have had this faith. I am not historically naïve enough to swallow unconditionally the New England version of American history. Many good and useful things didn't come over in the *Mayflower!* But I am willing to accept the claim that this peculiar American faith in education is, in the main, a product of the New England way. It was not notable, for instance, among the Dutch settlers; it was not notable in the South; despite Jefferson's ambitious plans for Virginia, it was not a mark of southern society until quite recent times. No, from the time Harvard College was founded to secure the survival of a learned ministry, to preserve in the new Cambridge the standards of the old, American education has had the mark of the Puritan upon it. On the whole that has been a good mark, but some of the problems of modern American educational policy come from the apparent irrelevance of that mark to modern conditions and from the survival of the faith in a world that has lost belief in the terms of the creed. For it would be dishonest to conceal the fact that American education began as a preparation for the next world. It was designed to make good Christians, not good citizens or subjects; the greater, it was assumed, included the less. Some of the problems of modern education in America come from the survival of the bias behind this tradition, while the tradition has been assailed and deeply altered by a tornado of winds of doctrine.

Of course, it is bad history to think of American education at any time as being wholly otherworldly. As Admiral Samuel Eliot Morison has shown, Harvard was never merely a seminary for ministers, the content of its curriculum never merely theological, the cultural pattern it attempted to impose never merely biblical. Harvard was a Renaissance as well as a Christian and semimedieval organization. Nor were the common schools of Massachusetts merely concerned to make good Christians; they aimed at a general culture usable in this world as well as serving as a preparation for the next. It would be absurd archaism to look back to a time when anywhere in what is now the United States public education paid no attention to worldly utility. Man does not live by bread alone, but he lives by bread all the same, and the founders of the dominant American educational tradition held firmly to this truth.

In my native land, Scotland, where the educational spirit and system has many things in common with the American spirit and system, all Scots children in the village schools were taught that the "chief end of man" was "to glorify God and to enjoy Him for-ever." But I shall not be letting you into any deeply guarded secret if I assert that the Scots have also managed to pay some attention to other lesser but still important ends of man and did not think the two sets of ends were incompatible. As the national bard puts it, "grace and gear" go together.

Nor could there be a more gross historical error than to see the education of the Middle Ages as entirely theological and nonutilitarian. If it differed from our system, it differed by being, if anything, more utilitarian, although the utility served was not identical with that we try to serve today. We shall get nowhere, that is to say, by lamenting the American attempt (which didn't begin with John Dewey or the triumph of Teachers College) to put education to work, to look for tangible results and those results as not being merely the higher cultivation of the individual. From the beginning, American education has attempted among other things—but probably predominantly—to serve social ends. It will continue to do so and it should continue to do so.

What social ends were to be served? They were the imposition or the insinuation of what may be called the New England spirit (although of course in other regions it had other names and slightly different aims). It aimed at producing a Bible-reading society, a society with common ethical standards, with a common attachment to local political institutions, with pride in local achievements, with loyalty to local interests. It is not so much that its aims differed greatly from those of the modern American public school as that it was only one of the institutions attempting to create a useful social ethos. It had as partner, not as rival, the church, and it had in the town meeting another form of public education in public virtue. Thus the great change in the position of the public school in America is not in what it has to do but in its arrival at the stage in which it has few aids in what it has to do. The trend of American education has been to put more and more public burdens on the school, to expect more and more of the school, but America always expected a lot of the school and has got a lot from the school. I think that one of the problems of modern American education is that too much is expected from the school, but if this is so it is an old story.

From the beginning the school in America has been a democratic force. I am aware of the social distinctions imported from England (and from other European countries) in the seventeenth and eighteenth centuries. I am aware of class distinctions at Harvard and of private tutors in Virginia. But the American school (using the term in its widest sense) has collaborated with other forces in American life in making for the kind of equality that I have already discussed briefly. The school has not set itself against the general trend of egalitarianism in American life; for some generations past is has—in its public version, at any rate—been a consciously democratizing force. This marks the American public school system off from some other systems giving almost as universal an introduction to elementary schooling. It was not the aim of the Prussian school system to produce or to aid democracy; its aim was to produce good subjects, good soldiers. It was the effect rather than the aim of the Scottish school system to promote political democracy. In France, after the Revolution, it was impossible—perhaps it still is impossible—to get a consensus as to what kind of society the public school system has aimed at promoting. At any rate, it has been impossible to get agreement on the kind of society it *should* aim at promoting.

The American school system has never, that is to say, tried to thwart the natural development of American society toward a system of minimal hereditary privilege and a system of maximum opportunity. To make possible the "career open to the talents," to foster the talents, to increase the opportunities of the average boy and girl, to give them the tools necessary for the full development and exploitation of their talents—these were and are the objectives of the American school system. They have been imitated as to aims and copied as to methods in many other countries (for example, in modern England) but America has been the pioneer.

But the American school has been, in the past century and in this one, called on to do more. It has not only been called on to make competent boys and girls; it has also been called on to make good American boys and girls. As I have already indicated, the early New England schools inculcated and supported the New England way . . . and that meant more than a church system. From the beginnings of the United States the schools were expected to make good Americans by precept and parable. Parson Weems and the great McGuffey were important makers of the American way of life. All societies live in great part by what it is not offensive to call myths. For much more than a century the American teacher and the American textbook have been creating and fostering helpful myths and thus helping to create and support "a more perfect union." Here, although the detailed aim was different, the American public schools, like the Prussian public schools, were part of the established political order. The orders differed, so did the aims and methods. But this function of the school was common to both systems.

There is no close historical parallel for another function of the American school system—one so important, so dominating, that it is natural that to it much should have been sacrificed and much should continue to be sacrificed even when, as now, the necessity is not so great. That function has been the making of Americans, the induction into the American way of life of the millions of the children of the immigrants who had come to the golden shore with, inevitably, inadequate preparation for a way of life very different from what they had known in Europe.

I have already alluded briefly to the great folk movement that poured tens of millions of immigrants into the United States in the nineteenth and twentieth centuries. It was one of the sources of American wealth and power, one of the proofs of American success, but it was also one of America's problems. Since the United States was based on a dogma laid down by the Founding Fathers in universal terms, it was easy enough to demand adherence to the principles of the American political system. Few doubted the premises or the promises of the Declaration of Independence or were unwilling to subscribe to them in good faith. But the formal adherence was not enough. How could the children of the immigrants in, for example, New England be made to feel the validity for *them* of the appeal to the New England past? Was the God of the early New Englanders their God, Plymouth Rock and Faneuil Hall their inheritance?

How could they be given the loyalty, the emotional attachment to the past that comes naturally to old societies where all share in the ancestral tradition of good and evil fortune? A defeat in common may be as unifying a memory as a victory in common (look at Ireland, look at the South), but the word to stress is *common*. In a deeper sense than probably was meant the old name for the public school system, the common school system, suggested a great national necessity. The children of the newcomers must be taken into the national tradition and it must be made real for them, part of their inheritance by training, by conditioning if not by blood. Of course, the problem was not uniquely American. In all the industrial countries of Europe, with populations drawn from the traditional life of the land, the schools were called on to make possible the adjustment to the modern, literate, mechanized life. Sherlock Holmes saw the London board schools as so many lighthouses, and some of the successes and failures of the American system can be paralleled in Europe.

Nor was the indoctrination of the young into a common

political belief and a common habit of political loyalty peculiar to America. It was one of the objects of the educational policy of the first French Republic with its insistence on a uniform language of instruction and the teaching of loyalty to the republic "one and indivisible." That France is now in her fifth republic suggests that this experiment in political education was not an unqualified success. In other European countries the school system was called on to create loyalties that did not come naturally, to make good Prussians out of Poles, good Germans out of Alsatians. In Ireland, so it is credibly reported, the so-called national schools taught the children to sing "I am a happy English child," but there is reason to believe that the political indoctrination of the Irish children was not complete.

In America it was. The patriotism of the children of the immigrants was not in any way inferior to the patriotism of the children of older stocks and the assimilation, through the school system, of the American patriotic tradition was complete. This is a success story and should be noted as such.

An even greater success story was the creation of a tradition in the new states of the Middle and Far West where all were immigrants, immigrants from Europe, immigrants from the East and from the South. The task was great, the need was great, the success was great. These pioneers, from Massachusetts and from Sweden, moving into the great, lone land had to be given emotionally potent links with the usable American past in the East and had to be given a usable American present. They had to be given a just pride in what they were doing and a just pride in what the ancestors of some of them had done—and that second pride had to be common to all. The common school had as its first purpose, or perhaps just after the mere conquest of illiteracy, the making of Americans and the creating of a common tradition. We all know the story of the college where a notice was put up: "This tradition goes into effect next Monday."

We all laugh; we should laugh. But something like that was done by the school system in the new states. It was done with success and it was worth doing.

Yet if this was the primary purpose of the school system it was obvious that certain alterations would have to be made in the means, since there was this alteration in the end. In the old traditional school system, largely exported and largely preserved in the East, especially in New England, there was a known, if expanding, body of knowledge that was to be imparted. Once primary school was passed, it was assumed that not all boys and girls would be up to the assimilation of this body of knowledge or would find any use for it if they did assimilate it. That everybody, barring the incurably moronic, should learn the "three R's" was one thing, that everybody should be offered whatever it was that "high school" connotated was another.

Much can be said against some of the innocent but not necessarily harmless illusions involved in the twentieth-century doctrine that no one should be refused as much higher education as he or she was willing to be exposed to. But socially, politically, there was and is a great deal to be said for the ideal if its real justification is allowed for; that justification, as I have suggested, is political, social rather than narrowly "educational." To keep boys and girls at school until eighteen so that they may become sharers in a common, although in some degree artificial, American tradition is a political good and an unmixed good if we do not deceive ourselves as to what we are doing. For remember that a generation ago many of those children, those adolescents who are "wasting their time," would have been on the coal breakers, down the mines, in backbreaking and not necessarily character-building labor on remote and miserable farms. The European observer contemplating an American high school ought to say, if he has any social and historical imagination, that here is a great and humane effort to make citizens and to save children from too-early contact with the necessary brutalities of life.

I shall even do what I have done elsewhere, defend the amount of time spent on games, on playing them, on watching them, on thinking about them. It is a lot of time. I lived for some months opposite a high school in an American city. I was, I must confess, a little astonished by the amount of time that seemed to be spent in standing around waiting for a bus to take teams and cheering squads off to some game or other. I did not, I must confess, think that all this standing and waiting was quite necessary or quite admirable. Yet some of the stress on sport is necessary and is admirable. Not because it builds up the bodies of the boys and girls—I am not sure that it does. At any rate, it does not train them in what is one of the oldest of human skills and is still a very useful one, the art of walking. But sport does unite in a common, deeply felt, and on the whole innocuous loyalty boys and girls (and parents) divided by a lot of barriers. Of course, the success of this unity by sport varies from place to place. It may not work very well on Manhattan Island or in other homes of the blackboard jungle.

Sport is the activity in which American race prejudice, still a national weakness, plays the smallest part. Sport is the easiest means of promotion. Outside the South, what basketball manager will turn down a seven-foot star because he is a Negro? What Harvard man would rather lose to Yale with a team of Lowells and Saltonstalls than win with a team of O'Briens and Konskis? This can be pushed too far. I think it is going too far to die for a college and I think that even star athletes should be required to learn to read and write.

Before I turn to the critical side, I should like to reaffirm my belief in the unifying force of the common high school. Here is the parallel to the Greek city festivals. Who that has seen the return of a victorious basketball team to a middle western town can fail to see the parallel?

> What little town by river or sea-shore
> . . . Is emptied of its folk, this pious morn?

The answer is scores, hundreds; they're off at the game. And if there is no

> . . . heifer lowing at the skies,
> And all her silken flanks with garlands drest?

there is the modern equivalent, the drum majorette.

But the Greeks to whom I have appealed not only preached and practiced what they called "gymnastic," they practiced what they called "music." They prized and rewarded intellectual achievement as they did physical achievement; they even prized it more. And it is the view of the current critics of the American school system that the American school system at all levels, from the primary school right through college, overdoes gymnastic and plays down music. I think the critics are right. I think that the social function of the school is overstressed and that the United States is now rich enough, unified enough, self-critical enough to ask more of the schools than that they should create a national ethos. It is mature enough, or ought to be mature enough, to be ready to ask the schools to lay less stress on making good, loyal Americans and more on making critical, technically competent citizens of a country that can no longer live to itself or be content with meeting its own self-created, historically justified but possibly obsolescent and dangerous standards. Again to harp on my implicit theme, the United States is living in a new, dangerous, unpleasant world and its educational system is in competition, as are all other sections of the American way of life. No one, I think, since Sputnik went into orbit doubts that.

All that I have described was useful, natural, defensible;

it still is. The social functions of the school, especially of the high school, are not at an end. But one result of the concentration on that social function was not so much the lowering as the abandonment of standards. What was thought to be "education" in a European secondary school or old New England academy was too narrow for the new world. It was too narrow because it did neglect some useful and new and necessary techniques of the new world. But it was too narrow also because, if the old standards had been insisted on, many, many pupils whom it would have been necessary to exclude from the formal instruction would also have been excluded, to the national loss, from the social molding. So studies had to be found that these pupils could master and possibly use later, which was all right. But these were deemed to be equal with studies that a smaller group could master and use. Typing was as good as trig. This was a practical and tolerable solution a generation ago, a necessary acceptance of facts about American life. But the American school system is no longer concerned with American life, but just with life . . . and death.

That the shock given to American complacency by the Russian triumph was healthy I suppose no one doubts. It was not only an awakening to a serious military danger; it was a firm suggestion to the American people to look at their educational system and to ponder both its defects and what can be done about them. It may be that by waking the American public from its undogmatic slumbers (in most cases it was plain slumber), Sputnik will rank with the shots at Lexington or Fort Sumter. It was certainly seen if not heard around the world.

What are the defects now being brought to the attention of the American parent? They are to some degree the reverse of the attractive medal to which I have called attention. If the main object of the school system is social and political, why should these aims be sacrificed to the mere pursuit of intellectual eminence? One answer is that among the urgent social and political aims of the United States at the present moment is survival in a highly competitive world, and that world cares little for the achievement of internal harmony in the United States and much for the distribution of mere material power. If the present school system is not producing an adequate supply of first-rate scientists and technicians, it is condemned for not doing a job that may be new but is one that must be tackled if the United States is to survive.

On the detailed criticisms of the curriculum, of the teachers, of the standards demanded and attained, I have nothing that is new and probably nothing that is valuable to say. Nevertheless, I shall say my piece. First of all, only a very rich country can afford a school system that takes so long to produce the finished product. In nearly all professions, possibly in all, the American finishes his professional training some years later than does his European opposite number. He may afford it in terms of money and the economy may afford it in terms of money, but can society afford it in terms of time? I wonder and I doubt. For the handful of absolutely top-flight and indispensable specialists perhaps the time is not too long. For the rest it is serious that entry into the productive field, whatever that field may be, should come so late. And it is so late because the boy and girl at the high school stage is not stretched enough.

I shall not inflict on you the current list of complaints. Why can't Johnny read? Why can't Sister count? Why can't Foreign Service officers speak foreign languages? Why do high schools aim so low in such vital fields as mathematics and physics? Why have colleges to do so much of what, in other countries, is regarded as schoolwork? I think all these questions are relevant, all contain some elements of just criticism. The justification of the social function of the common school that I have already given does not mean that schools could not try harder and ask their pupils to try harder. Effort is not un-American; this is recognized in sport, and if schoolwork could be given some of the prestige of games, of the teams, even of the band, there might be less to complain about. In an account of life in a progressive college for young women, Randall Jarrell makes a German professor recall that the Emperor William II once expressed alarm that German parents were ruining their children's eyesight by encouraging them to work too hard at school. He went on to say that no educational system did more to protect the pupils' eyesight than the American—an unkind but not, I think, totally unjust remark.

James Bryant Conant has been inspecting the high schools of the country and has published his findings. I am in total agreement with everything that the report suggests in the way of improving the curriculum and of distinguishing between the pupils who are doing what I may be allowed to call "real" schoolwork and those who are being prepared for the unexamined life. The really bright boy and girl is the victim of the present school system and he or she must be delivered from the lockstep of promotion by age or the temptations of snap courses, as well as from the positive deprivation of good teaching given by teachers who are not tied by their own limitations to the textbook and can keep abreast and ahead of the class. If this means rethinking the function of schools of education, I am all for it.

But a European observer, especially an observer from England, will be struck by the fact that even after the Conant program is put into effect the pupil in the American high school is not going to be overworked or, if you like to put it that way, equipped to enter on university work as soon as he might be. Even after the Conant reforms, colleges will still be doing what is in France or England thought to be schoolwork. To avoid any imputation of displaying the condescension attributed to foreigners I may say that I am far from enamored of the results of the English system. We specialize too early and if our specialization produces some brilliant specimens who leave school fit to enter the junior class of a good American university, it also produces one-sided and intellectually crippled specimens who leave the university less fit for a higher education than when they entered it, victims of a system that encourages specialization from the age of fourteen and assumes that a bright boy will pick up all the surrounding knowledge that he needs to make him an educated man.

But if *we* assume, too easily and in face of the evidence, that plunging a boy into what may be a narrow specialization at an age when his curiosity ought to be wide and welcoming is a prudent proceeding, *you,* it seems to me, fall victims to what is, I firmly believe, the great American educational superstition. That is the belief that all that must be learned need be or, indeed, can be taught. It is my view that a great deal of what we need to learn we can learn only by doing, by *really* doing, not by simulating doing in school, that many problems can only be dealt with as they arise, that many problems cannot be reduced to terms of courses and textbooks. And my final heresy is that we must enter life with the knowledge that there are problems, as yet unknown, that we shall fail to solve, that what we are promised is the right to the pursuit of happiness, not happiness itself. (I have been told that the constitution of California promises happiness, but, then, California is outside normal human calculation.)

Behind the weakness of the high school curriculum, behind the weakness of much of the college curriculum, lies the belief that the school in its widest sense must take over all that the church, the town meeting, and the family did in the past, the belief that the good American is the successful applier of recipes for success and happiness learned at school and college or by postal refresher courses. What is the relevance of this belief to the burning question of the curriculum? First of all, it helps to account for the "democratic" character of the curriculum, for the equalization in formal merit of math and washing machine management. You will seldom have to use math—look at all the little reckoners you can buy—you will have to know how to run the washing machine or whatever other gadget is in question. To insist, nevertheless, that if a high school has got to choose it had better choose math or Latin is to be undemocratic. It is to insist that some things are superior to others and, in turn, that fewer people can master these than can master the techniques of mechanical living. I do not deny the importance of the machine aids to gracious living. But they can be bought; the art of running them can be learned easily. The boy who majors in filling station skills and even the girl who majors in cookery (a more fundamental and more serious art) are, from the school's point of view, a less important investment than the one who can handle concepts or can see why a machine works or why proteins are necessary to a good diet. It is not the main business of the school to prepare a boy or girl simply to earn his living or even to be a good American in the patriotic sense. At any rate, it is wrong to make this so much the aim of the school system that the exceptional boy or girl is never stretched and for that reason may never know or want to use the full potentialities of his or her talent.

Even for the average boy, even for the less than average boy, the attempt to substitute for the home, the church, and society in general has its dangers. The case for the religious neutrality of the American public school is overwhelmingly strong, but it is, I think, an illusion that because it would be dangerous or impossible to fill the gap made by the decline of formal belief (I do not say of formal or real religion) the gap is not there. To be silent on the greatest questions of human destiny is necessary, since we are not agreed on the answers, but it leaves the questions to be felt, even by the dull, as unanswered. It is wrong, then, to suggest that the school system can or should answer all the questions that an adolescent or even a young man or woman will put to the universe. Perhaps no school system can, but certainly an officially neutral system can't.

What can it do? First of all, I think, in the present crisis it should not educate the pupil "for the world he is going to live in." We don't know what kind of world he is going to live in; all that we can be certain of is that, during a normal lifetime, the world will change in ways we can't now foresee. What we can do is to suggest that the world will change, and give intellectual tools for understanding that truth, intellectual prophylaxis against the provincialism which suggests that only the most obviously current problems are the real problems. (Sputnik merely called attention to certain defects in American education; it did not create the defects.) Unless at least the more intelligent pupils are given some critical habits (including the habit of not believing all that their teachers tell them), we can be sure of one thing. They will not be at home in the world, the unknown world they are going to live in, and no textbooks, no courses, no Advice to the Lovelorn columns are going to help very much. Education would benefit in efficiency and prestige if it were more modest and more presumptuous, if it refused to claim to do so much and insisted on a hierarchy of values in what it can do.

There may be an apparent paradox in my now insisting on the encouragement of the critical spirit after applauding the success of the school system in breeding loyalty and in creating a common tradition. But it is an inevitable danger that the necessary solutions of one age are carried over to another. What the American school system did a generation ago was necessary (and the United States could afford the wasteful elements in the solution), but today I doubt that it is necessary and that the United States can afford so much waste of time which is waste of brains.

In what sense and in what directions should the critical

spirit be encouraged? Here I will begin by making a concession to the ideal of national unity. I do not suggest that the American school set out to disabuse its pupils of admiration for the American way of life. If the formation of a united nation is no longer the primary task of the schools, the formation of a disunited nation is certainly no legitimate object for a school system. It is possible to encourage the critical spirit and yet to be nearly sure that the end product will be a deeper and more intelligent appreciation of American life rather than a simple admiration for everything in America merely because it is "American." (After all, that involves admiring very different and often inconsistent things.) For the bright boy or girl, what the school can profitably do is to give him or her the habit of looking at contemporary social and political problems with the rule of judgment in his mind, not only that the American way can sometimes be wrong but also that the world, rightly or wrongly, is not necessarily destined to go the American way—at any rate, not if the blind force of things is simply left to take its course.

The pupil who has been forced to stretch himself, who because he is bright has been steered away from snap courses and quick and easy answers, should be given the habit of waiting before he makes up his mind, even in a patriotic and American direction. He should most certainly not be given the idea that we know already how the world must go, that we have a plan given to us that history must follow. One of the most dangerous illusions of the Communist world is that they have such a plan, and one of the dangers to world peace that most alarms me is the confidence that this belief breeds and the temptation that it offers to bend history, past and future, to fit the plan. The American high school pupil of the brighter type should leave school with certain intellectual tools that he can use and with an intellectual attitude incompatible with the easy belief that there is an answer ready for all questions, or even that we know what the questions will be to which we, individually and nationally, will want answers. The time for just making Americans is over, or, at any rate, it is not the only job of the schools; the time for the making of the critical and open-minded citizen has arrived.

I confess that my ideas on the school problem are orthodox, are exterior, and lack concreteness. When I move on to the higher education I am not more confident in my solutions but more confident that I understand and—what is equally important—feel the problems. I have studied at Harvard and taught at Yale, which Harvard men will think is the proper order, and I have taught at and studied in operation American universities and colleges of very different types. The first thing that I feel has to be said about them is that the aim of the American college, even more than the aim of the American high school, is peculiarly American. Elsewhere the college, the university, is seen as by definition the possession of a small minority. The number of people likely in any generation to profit by a higher education is limited, it is believed, not by money (though that has played a great part in the past) but by the niggardliness of nature. There are comparatively few people fit to be university students; there are fewer fit to be university teachers. American theory and practice have denied both these European dogmas. In the American context it has been right to do so. But it should be noted that one implication of the denial is that what in Europe we think of as the content of the higher education is absurdly limited—that if we teach people what they are willing to learn, the number of people who are fit to be taught will increase to meet the proportionately increased number of people who are fit to teach. At first sight, this is an academic version of Parkinson's Law, that work expands to fill up the time that is available in which to do it, and I will not conceal my conviction that there is a great deal of waste effort in the American higher education (and in all higher education). There remains not only the problem of the students who can't even learn what they want to learn but also the problem of whether a four-year college course is not a horribly wasteful way of teaching even simple crafts, even teaching life adjustment, and whether the four-year course does not postpone until too late the actual meeting with life as apart from the theoretical adjustment to it.

Probably no great harm is done, except in encouraging a national indifference to excellence as distinguished from competence by the proliferation of colleges, degrees, professors, doctors. And the educational system doesn't create the indifference to excellence; it only reflects it. But if no great harm is done neither is any great good done by giving Ph.D.'s in physical education or in educational method. Possibly there may, every few years or so, be a really new discovery in physical education, a really new discovery in education, not simply a rearrangement of existing data tricked out as a contribution to learning. I cannot help remembering that Knute Rockne taught chemistry not physical education, that Robert Kiphuth of Yale is not a Ph.D., and that the famous young man who said that he would die for dear old Rutgers would have been surprised if he had been told that he would get a posthumous Ph.D. if he did so. To be brief and frank, a great deal of the higher education in America is an education designed to soothe envy, to gratify social ambition, to train manipulators of not very difficult techniques. This process probably increases happiness; it less certainly increases efficiency; it does not lie at the center of the American educational problem.

What does? What does lie there is the training of the comparatively small number of persons capable not necessarily of making original contributions but of understanding original contributions. You Americans have got hold of the right end of one stick, a business of universities and colleges is to provide men and women of a high degree of critical competence for public life, for business, for education, for many things other than the life of learning or of adding to learning. As Harvard produced more than learned ministers, the modern American university should produce more than scholars and scientists; it should create an intelligent, critical, competent working elite.

But it should also produce those scholars and scientists, and here it is that the American university should not express the spirit of contemporary America but should run counter to it. It will hardly be argued that the present temper of America is critical; it is fearful, which is not the same thing. There is enough truth in the picture of the "organization man," of the pursuit of "adjustment," of "togetherness," to make it a primary duty of the university to exalt, to reward, to protect the nonorganization man. This involves protecting cranks and men who go up the wrong alley and stay there for a lifetime. It involves a lot of waste in deciding who are the independent spirits that deserve protection as well as need it. We can be certain that many mistakes will be made, that the incompetent as well as the malevolent will work their way in, past test oaths and efficiency ratings. You may demand "publication," "research," but you can't—effectively—demand original research and worthwhile publication. You can only be glad when you have got them.

There is another way in which the duty of the American universities at the present time is to set themselves against the current of opinion and that is in emphasizing that there are many things in the world that can't be settled in terms of the price system. There are many things which we can recognize as valuable but which we cannot price and which we cannot expect the price system to produce. Some of these are what is loosely called "cultural goods," but, again harping on the world series into which the United States has been projected, some of them are conditions of national survival. If we still believe that what is good for General Motors is good for the United States we doom the United States to defeat, for there are many things good and necessary for the United States that are no use at all to General Motors. The businessman has his place and it is an important, highly respectable and highly rewarded place, but in the modern world he is not to be taken too seriously . . . a society that takes him too seriously will go the way of Carthage and Venice—but faster.

It is probable but not proved that the United States produces more inspired gadgeteers than any other country. Yankee ingenuity is not a myth. But is it heresy to suggest that what the United States needs today is more basic curiosity, not only about what can be done but about what should be done, than an Edison or a Ford ever displayed? In the kind of conflict in which we are engaged, the improvisers, the tinkerers, the patient experimenters in a narrow field are indispensable, but they are less indispensable (if the comparison can logically be permitted) than the visionaries, than the people who ask why grass is green and not how much tail fin the American public can be induced to pay for.

The world we live in is in danger from the fruits of the original ideas of men who are not to be found or developed by the ordinary demands of business and who do not, as a rule, flourish in its atmosphere. Perhaps this highly relevant truth would be better appreciated if the average American reflected how comparatively little the United States has contributed to the basic scientific ideas of the world. (I think that Cambridge University has done more that way than the whole United States.) It would also be profitable to reflect that of the most world-changing inventions of the past two generations only one, the airplane, is a 100 per cent American achievement.

The American university has here a function that the

American school has not, that is, to discover, train, foster, reward the comparatively small number of men and women in each generation who have new ideas: new technical ideas, new scientific ideas, new philosophical ideas. The Wright brothers were more important than Henry Ford or Thomas Alva Edison. But more important than any of them were the great makers of modern physical theory. And it is not only the scientists. I question whether any of his contemporaries affected the world more than did Karl Marx. I don't like the way he did it, but it is the beginning of wisdom to notice that he did it.

We want a picture of the world that enables the American to escape from his limited picture of how even the American world was made, that allows for the role of mere curiosity, for Newton and his apple, for the reflection on received ideas that led to the doctrines of John Maynard Keynes whose ideas affect us more than those of any millionaire of his generation, for the great artists who have made the world seem intelligible and tolerable. To insist on this truth at this moment and to do its share in making the acceptance of this truth fruitful is the first duty of the American university. That asserting this truth will lead to some undemocratic corollaries is, I fear, true. But I have already given my adherence to the view that "democratic" is a political term, that there are many things in life not to be settled by numbers or by the price system or by asking "Do they make people feel good?" In our war with the weapons of the spirit we do right to remind ourselves that

> Thy friends are exultations, agonies
> And love, and man's unconquerable mind.

The duty of the universities and colleges of America is to fill that mind with ideas and resources adequate to our age and the most important of these is the ability to see what the problems of this age are and what of the national past is relevant to them. To do that effectively, we must abandon a certain dislike of "undemocratic" superiority in mental equipment. We must be prepared to give exceptional people exceptional educational treatment. If justice is mere equality, we must be prepared to be unjust. If this be treason, make the most of it.

5

The Character of American Culture

"Culture" is a highly ambiguous term. However I may limit my definition of it, "culture" remains a wide term demanding for its full definition and illustration a range of knowledge that I do not possess.

Culture can have two meanings. There is the meaning given to the word by the anthropologist, in which all social habits, techniques, religious practices, marriage customs, in fact everything—including the kitchen sink—is examined to throw light on how a particular society lives and moves, or just exists. Then there is "culture" in a narrower sense, in which we are concerned not with material techniques, not with the social organization that holds society together, but with the ideas, the aesthetic experiences and achievements, and the philosophical or religious ideas that affect and are affected by the aesthetic experiences and achievements of a given society. A special variant of the last sense of "culture" is the narrow identification of the word with the fine arts and the implicit relegation of the fine arts to the margin of life, to what is done in leisure or for leisure.

None of these usages of the word is strictly separable from the others. The first usage obviously includes all the possible variations on the meaning and even the most restricted implies the wider meaning as a background. I shall not try, therefore, to attain a rigorous standard of definition or eschew all overlapping of one definition of culture and another. I shall try to deal with the problem of the level and the tone of American culture in its second sense, but I shall not try to define that second sense narrowly or regard myself as debarred from using illustrations from American life that a culture snob would think showed a confusion of ideas or a lowering of standards. In my view culture that is merely a set of aesthetic practices, merely exemplified in private or even in public taste, is a theme of importance—to be treated by somebody else. What I am concerned with is the problem of cultural standards and achievements in an advanced democratic society, specifically the United States. And that cultural achievement cannot be separated from religion, education, the character of the state, the general aims and ambitions of American society.

To fall back on one of my devices already used, what is the cultural "mark" of American society? It is the absence of a strong, received aristocratic tradition, on the one side, and, on the other, the presence of a number of what can loosely, in a social if not a purely political sense, be called "democratic" biases and practices. The fine arts, literature, music, the content of the higher education have from the beginning been affected by the general egalitarian, progressive, optimistic, factual, future-discounting tone of American life. As I shall have occasion to note later, this bias of American life has often produced a powerful reaction and some of the classics of American literature are in the nature of minority protests against just those marks of American society that I have stressed. Nevertheless, American culture, in its widest sense, has these marks and American culture in its narrower sense has them too, even if to many the marks appear as scars.

What in the beginning marked off the nascent American culture from that of Europe? One thing I would suggest was poverty, poverty in a society already more egalitarian than that of Europe. People came to America to get rich (among other reasons); they did not arrive rich. Establishing their culture beachheads on the eastern coast, they had not the resources of time or of energy for the reproduction on the American shore of the elaborate cultural life that some of them had shared and all of them had heard of in Europe. There was no demand for a Vandyke, an Inigo Jones, a Milton in seventeenth-century America; no means of producing or sustaining such artists.

The contrast with Spanish America is striking in at least one field, that of architecture. The Spanish colonists had two resources that the English colonists lacked: a docile and utilizable Indian population and "treasure," gold and silver. There was from the first in Spanish America a surplus for the fine arts. There was more. There was a government and a church that both aimed at splendor and had the political resources to use the surplus to produce it. It was not only that in English America there were no easily exploitable human and material resources to permit the creation of a materially splendid society. There were no institutions to insist that such splendor should be provided. The royal government, the churches could not, even if they had wished, force the colonists to produce art works on the scale of the Cathedral of Mexico.

Dwelling houses, churches and public buildings were necessarily simple, utilitarian. They could be and sometimes were aesthetically satisfactory as well, but the aim was not splendor. It was utility. Simplicity often is a form of beauty and elegance, but I think that some harm is done to the modern American sense of the beautiful by too much insistence on the triumphs of a simplicity that was imposed by need rather than by choice. From the beginning beauty was associated in American experience with functional fitness. It is an admirable association and, if one has to choose, it is better to have functional fitness than irrelevant ornament, but a certain Puritanical indifference or hostility to mere beauty, mere ornament is or was part of the American inheritance.

"Puritanical." I am aware that the word is ambiguous and I have no intention of using it as a term of abuse. But it did matter that the predominant religious tradition of early English America was one that left little place for the "luxe pour Dieu" that produced the great cathedrals and abbeys of Europe. I am aware that English (and American) Puritans had a high and competent sense of the place of music in divine worship. Nevertheless, the new environment was not that provided by Rome for Palestrina or by Leipzig for Bach. Milton was a musically minded Puritan poet, but he would not have found much to gratify his tastes had he emigrated to New England or to Virginia.

And if the material and ideological obstacles to the transfer of the more lavish, extravagant and nonutilitarian forms of the arts to America did not work so effectually in the case of literature, the transfer had some special difficulties all the same. One was material; there was, again, no means of accumulating an economic surplus to support the career of letters. It was possible to export the old classical learning and equally important the old and new biblical learning and, what was more important, the Bible itself. And no people that had the Bible made available and treasured by the established order was cut off from the highest literary excellence. Yet again the colonies—with no theaters, no court, no court patronage, as yet no equivalent of the new academies like the Royal Society of London, with the new life constantly calling for new effort, with no leisure class—could not be expected to and did not produce a variegated, nonutilitarian, original culture in the arts or, indeed, in the sciences, in what was then called natural philosophy. It would be absurd to make this a matter of reproach. It was part of the price paid for the establishment of the peculiar and successful Anglo-American society out of which the United States and its present culture have come. All I should like to suggest is that there was a necessary price; it was paid.

I am now coming to a more controversial part of my subject, the character of this necessarily democratic culture. That the American culture, on its aesthetic and intellectual side, is democratic I shall try to show later. What I want to do at the moment is to stress its early nonaristocratic character. The European culture from which it stemmed had its democratic elements: its folk ballads dealing with the woes and happiness of the "lower orders," the "short and simple annals of the poor." It had in its material works of art plenty of scenes from vulgar life, on the porches of great cathedrals, or the illuminations of the *Hours* of the Duc de Berry. But the more splendid forms of artistic achievement in the Middle Ages, as in the Renaissance, were aristocratic. The great popular legends were of kings and queens, of princes and princesses, of knights, of crusades and battles, feuds in castles, not of their less interesting equivalents in cottages. No doubt there are signs of a protest against this concentration on the great. The Robin Hood legend is an example. But most people accepted the distinction. Poor French peasants passed on, with faith and admiration, the legend of the Four Sons of Aymon and even now it is legends of the higher feudalism that Sicilian peasants paint on their carts. They would have agreed with Calpurnia:

> When beggars die, there are no comets seen;
> The heavens themselves blaze forth the death of princes.

Now, the settlers brought out from Europe, more specifically from the British Isles, this aristocratic culture. (The Bible, after all, is full of kings and nobles; sinners most of them, but interesting sinners. The metaphorical language of the Bible is royal, not democratic.) But in the American environment the aristocratic culture, accepted and admired by the people, began to wither. The old ballads were brought over but were transformed, given an American, frontier-bred, forest-bred character. The legends of kings and princes became legends of men of the people winning the endless war against the wilderness and the Indian. Robin Hood was a hero that could be transported to the frontier; Richard Coeur de Lion was not.

I attach great importance to the creation of this frontier folk epic, not only because it tells us of the formation of the modern American culture but because it is the greatest American cultural export. It should be remembered that it is English America that has produced the only universally accepted new epic theme. The "matter of America" is in the true succession from the "matter of France" (Roland and the Paladins) and the "matter of Britain" (King Arthur and the Knights of the Round Table).

It is a matter not of kings and great nobles but of the self-made men of the forest and later of the prairie; it is a democratic epic theme. As far as there is a genuine American national tradition of legend, this is it. I am not altogether convinced that scholars, as well as hard-pressed men of letters, have not invented some of the prestige of the frontier heroes. I know how the Buffalo Bill legend was created; I have suspicions about Paul Bunyan and Mike Fink; but even if the legend has undergone the shaping hand of the poet or the poetaster or the scholar, that is how great legends are given their final and effective traditional form. And the legend of the West is still living in America—and still exportable to Europe. The conquest of the TV screen by the West is conclusive proof of the power of the legend that for a time represented a fact and for longer met a need of the new American social culture, a need for heroes and heroic deeds in an American and egalitarian context. I should not assert that as an art form the way in which this legend has been given to the American public is one of the greatest human achievements. I doubt if even Fenimore Cooper as a writer is in the class of his model, Scott. But the legend he launched on the world was unlike the legend Scott exported to Europe and America, a modern living legend with a future. It was a legend of heroes chosen not by birth but by themselves.

As far as American literary culture has been the embodiment of this heroic legend it has been one of the makers and the marks of the American national ethic. And I, for one, am not disposed to look this gift horse too closely in the mouth or to assess this national asset in a purely literary crucible. If (as I think is true) the American national hero who is most effectively cast in the epic mold and most excites the national curiosity, as well as admiration, is Lincoln, the lesson is reinforced, for here is the folk hero, coming from the folk, embodying in the highest power their possibilities of promotion and achievement. That is one way in which American culture is democratic.

There is another, one that is perhaps less edifying, less a pure acquisition. In a famous passage in his book on Hawthorne, Henry James stresses and laments the poverty of resources available to the American man of letters. Compared to his European brother, how little he has to use, how simple the social structure in which he is to set the characters! There is something comic in this long list of things that America has not got. It is, oddly enough, the converse of what Goethe had to say: he congratulated America on its escape from the feudal past that James coveted. And obviously James exemplified in his own work the possibilities of the new American theme contrasted with the old, traditional European themes. But there was something in the Jamesian lament, if not quite what James thought it was.

For in the more sophisticated forms of literary art, the egalitarian bias of American life worked against the reception of the more subtle forms of art by the great American public—and there was no substitute for the great American public. There was no center of patronage, of support, of protection for the artist.

It is not necessary to swallow all the criticisms of American society fashionable with writers for over a hundred years—criticisms of the aridity of American culture, of the dry, inhospitable air in which the artist found it difficult to breathe—to recognize that, for some types of artist at any rate, nineteenth-century America—busy building itself up, completing the conquest of the frontier, assimilating the vast immigrant floods—could not be, or at any rate was not, very hospitable to the arts.

It was perhaps not accidental that the "golden day" of New England marked not the first efflorescence of a culture but the sunset of the old, learned, theocratic New England way of life, the marriage of the old Puritan conscience with the optimism of the Enlightenment. Emerson, Hawthorne, and the lesser men, Holmes, Lowell and the rest, were fruits of a society declining and which owed its charm and some of its force to its nearly twilight character. There is something paradoxical in this situation and it is a paradox that many Americans refuse to face, but there it is. The New England culture, the best integrated, the most internally harmonious regional culture that America has known, knew its golden day only when its decline was imminent. "Minerva's owl flies only in the dusk," said Hegel, and this deep saying applies to Boston, Concord, Salem. And—a banality that I am almost ashamed to utter—the great figures of American literary culture have been on the whole hostile to or at any rate highly critical of American life. Emerson had his repeated bursts of optimism but the world in which he spent the second half of his life was a world that listened not at all to his deepest message. It is hardly necessary to stress the pessimism of Hawthorne or the ostentatious disillusionment of Henry Adams.

And it was not only the New Englanders who were disillusioned, cut off. Whitman alone kept his spirits up and it is to be doubted if his best poetry is really to be found in those paeans to the spirit of democracy, those laudations of "Pioneers, O Pioneers." For Mark Twain the human situation was incurably tragic and for Melville the human illusion inevitably led to a dead end. "Round the world! There is much in that sound to inspire proud feelings, but whereto does all that circumnavigation conduct? Only through numberless perils to the very point whence we started, whence those we left behind secure, were all the time before us." Could there be a more un-American attitude than Melville's (and there are other lessons to the same effect)?

Classical American literature is not notably "useful" in the narrow nationalist sense. It is useful in a deeper sense, as is any penetrating, truthful, moving insight into the human situation. But the average American—optimistic, energetic, convinced, despite Melville, that circumnavigation does conduct us somewhere and somewhere worth arriving at—was and is naturally put off by the insistence on the darker side of the American situation. He has too often despised and distrusted the artist who has reciprocated the attitude. Exiled even if he did not leave the territorial bounds of the United States, the artist, the philosopher, the pure scientist were both cut off and cut themselves off from the main, cheerful stream of national tradition.

Of course, the alienation of the artist was not purely an American problem. War on the bourgeoisie, on bourgeois ideals and practices, was one of the common slogans of European life, especially in France. But Dickens and Hugo, social critics as they were, were not cut off from the life of their age as were their American opposite numbers and they were and have remained effective national heroes as no American author, not even Mark Twain, has been.

The consequence has been a separation of what I am prepared to call the higher culture and the less original, more perishable, more optimistic, more American (in the patriotic sense) culture that has unfortunate results even today—or especially today.

Here it is necessary to say something of the picture of the American cultural past that American academics have been presenting not so much to the public as to the captive audiences of the colleges. Nothing could be more admirable from a moral as well as an intellectual point of view than the industry and the acuteness and probity with which American scholars have examined all the American past, the works of the great, the near great, and the merely "interesting." But here I take my life in my hands and, as a foreigner, I should like to suggest that in their desire to assess accurately the American cultural past they have tended to stress its utility for the American student to an excessive degree. The ordinary, intelligent, interested but not totally fascinated young man or woman who is introduced to the idea of literature as more than a mere diversion, as an illumination of life and not as a mere distraction from it, may find the great American classics depressing and the lesser lights, so laboriously resurrected or at any rate exhumed, both mediocre and boring. American literary culture is not varied enough (is especially not rich enough in first-class poetry) to provide adequate nutriment for the young.

In a legitimate attempt to prove the original value of the American contribution American critics and scholars, it seems to me, have tended to put blinkers round their charges, who might otherwise look out at the great world and discover there much that is profound, illuminating, and nourishing, even for Americans, but which has the handicap of having been written not by Americans nor for Americans but by human beings for human beings. It was the advantage of the old classical curriculum on which the New England masters were brought up that it enforced knowledge of nonnational, of remote types of human achievement, that it insinuated the idea of a common human experience that Homer and Vergil threw light on. Today only the Bible (as far as it is still read apart from being bought) performs that function.

Something of the same limitation arises in the study of other aspects of American culture. It was a misfortune that the great expansion of the United States, in area, in wealth, in ambition, came at a time when in all countries of the new machine world taste was at its lowest, most timid, least connected with the forces of real creation. It is not only in the United States that money was squandered in atrocious imitations of the "Gothic," in inappropriate revivals of the classical, in ingenious and learned but not very relevant exercises in the Romanesque. To repeat, the United States was not the only sufferer. Is there any worse piece of church building erected regardless of cost anywhere in the United States than the Sacré-Coeur in Montmartre? Germany, France, and England are full of railway stations, government buildings, town halls that cannot be exceeded for unbeautiful ingenuity in any American city. (And I have some peculiarly unlucky American cities in mind.) Yet in the European cities, as a rule, the past had left achievements that ought to have put the modern architects and patrons to shame.

In many American cities there was nothing to offset the extravagantly outrageous taste of the gilded age—or later. Of course, there were pioneers like Louis Sullivan and many American cities have buildings of the late nineteenth and the early twentieth century that architects from Europe go on pilgrimage to. But visually the United States boomed at a bad time. And we have here, I think, another cause of alienation between the American and the higher culture of his country and age.

What of it? Is his situation any worse than that of the representative Englishman or Frenchman? Do they admire and use the products of the highest culture in their age and country? Of course not. But the American is in a special position. He is in Henry James's America, where the background to the arts has to be created and assimilated, where democratic judgment is part of the national ethos, where reverence is a quality reserved for a few sacred political slogans and institutions, where the not totally harmful snob values of an aristocratic culture are absent. The American is left to himself, not only because he does not accept leaders but because many leaders will not lead. For that reason, and possibly for others, the American cultural scene is peculiarly divided, the national unity, so remarkable at other levels, is here almost totally missing.

On the one hand, the American willingness to try anything once aids the arts, aids the preacher of new aesthetic or social doctrine. Just as American law tolerates, to a degree that surprises the European visitor, unorthodox systems of medicine, just as every known form of religious belief gets a welcome, so every new form of the arts, every new theory, every new form of practice finds buyers, in both a financial and a psychological sense. If from one point of view America suffers by having no accepted standards of excellence, she gains in another by not being hidebound by accepted standards of excellence. The very absence of what I may call "normative" institutions is a blessing. At any rate, it may seem so when the role of the French Academy in one field and the English Royal Academy in another is contemplated.

Probably at no time in history has the seller of cultural gods had it so good, in the sense that buyers will not be choked off by a mere inability to understand what it is all about. In face of the claims of the new art forms, in literature, in music, in painting, in sculpture, even in architecture, millions of Americans act like so many Texans afraid not to buy a potential oil well. What is offered may be unintelligible and unattractive, but it may conceal a gusher all the same. (I hasten to say that I am not describing buyers who are looking for a cash capital gain, but buyers in the widest sense of the term, who do not want to miss what may be the great cultural revelation of the age.)

This hospitality applies not only to the arts but to other aspects of culture, and notably to religion and what may be called philosophy. The American who seeks deliverance in analysis or in some new psychological school, who wants to master Zen Buddhism in ten easy lessons is a direct descendant of the seekers after knowledge whom Emerson made fun of more than a century ago—but who provided Emerson with a great part of his audiences and readers. It is not the searching after new things that is new, it is the evaporation, in the century since the decline of the Transcendentalists, of the old orthodoxy against which Emerson and his brethren reacted.

Here, again, the American situation is not unique. All over the Western world the seekers are as numerous as in St. Paul's Athens and the doctrines offered are much more varied. I am reduced to uttering a platitude when I stress the speed and diversity of change in our contemporary world. Our picture of it is changing so fast that it is vain to look for a central core of doctrine round which we can arrange our cultural life. If the modern world has such a core, a central and triumphant discipline, it is in physics, and who that is not quite a respectable mathematician can even begin to grasp what the physicists are doing? We can grasp in general what their allies and pupils, the engineers, are doing. Each new satellite, each new threat of more murderous rocketry, keeps them in our mind and we know that they can provide the means for destroying us. We are all in the

Western world in the same cultural boat, in a world we never made where old patterns are dissolving and changing too fast for us to adjust easily or comfortably or even to decide what we should adjust to.

But what is different in the American situation is first of all the democratic tradition of culture which I have briefly described. The old traditional order of a "higher" culture handed down from above—representing overtly aristocratic values or, at any rate, being based on the premise that some forms of culture are superior to others and that superiority is not simply an aspect of their popularity—is probably dying in Europe. But it is not yet dead. It visibly survives in the curriculum of the schools, in the prestige still attached to traditional hierarchical values, and (this is a matter where nothing but intuition can be relied on) in a genuine humility before the claims of the traditional culture that produces a willingness to learn that in turn results, in a good many cases, in a genuine conversion to the standards of a higher culture and a genuine appreciation of its products.

It is true that this acceptance of the traditional culture, this docile readiness to be initiated into it as far as natural talents and acquired knowledge make it possible, is not quite that immersion in the highest things that the preachers of culture, Matthew Arnold and T. S. Eliot, have meant. Nevertheless, the attitude preserves the older culture long enough for it to be possible to hope that a new culture, fusing the best of old and new, may arrive before general barbarism does.

The 800,000 copies of a translation of the *Odyssey* sold in England may not represent a genuine readiness to put oneself in the way of understanding of a remote way of life or a willingness to see and feel the human situation in another form from that to which we are habituated. But they do represent something that, faced with the products of the lower culture, with rock 'n' roll and the comics, we may be inclined to forget does exist.

If (as I think is the case) much of the pessimism of the "intellectuals" in America, in Britain, in Europe, arises from the collapse of the hopes based on the democratization of society, the end of the belief that the only things needed to win the masses to the higher culture were leisure, abundance, more "education," cheap books as well as the novel possibilities of radio and TV, then it is worth while to remind ourselves that not all those hopes were vain.

It is even more dangerous to blind ourselves to the facts of our situation (here I include both Britain and the United States in a common dilemma). We can do this in a new way as well as in the old way that asserted that we all must needs love the better when we see it. We can persuade ourselves that the new popular art forms are the natural successors of the old art forms, that they represent an inevitable adjustment to a new form of society. Thus rock 'n' roll is a necessary reflection of contemporary malaise; Li'l Abner, the equivalent of the great popular authors of the past, of Mark Twain and Dickens. If the boys and girls who pour out from high schools don't want to read, in a sense can't read, the reflection is on the absurd prestige we attach to reading or on the absurd and irrelevant reading matter issued to the aspiring young and their turning to other art forms than literature.

There is some plausibility in all these defenses of abdication in favor of popular adolescent taste. I think it likely that the literary arts may be giving way in prestige, perhaps in cultural utility, to other arts, to the plastic arts and, above all, to music. Music, I think, has become the refuge of the intelligent man and woman today and that not because hi-fi has enabled him to gratify his tastes but because those tastes have produced the market for hi-fi. I think that a timid reverence for "classics" may mean that school reading programs have a diseducative effect, since serious reading becomes associated with boredom. And in any group of intelligent boys and girls there are sure to be young men and young women of whom some have no more an eye for reading than others have an ear for music, or others the ability to do simple sums.

But the present cultural crisis is not concerned with these cases. It is right to discriminate among comics, to point out the superiority of "Li'l Abner" over records of violence, empty of ideas, for example. It is right to insist on the technical superiority of a great jazz performer like Louis Armstrong over the current wailers and moaners. These last may enable a great many of the young to express themselves vicariously, but it is a dangerous extension of democratic prejudice to assert that all forms of self-expression are commendable or equally admirable and promising. It is wrong and a "treason of the learned" to exalt the art forms that are most popular today simply because they are popular in merely numerical terms. "Dare to be a Daniel" was the message of a popular hymn. "Dare to be a square" is a motto I should like to see adopted by more academics and other ex officio molders of the public mind.

The reasons why this motto is not adopted are various. One is the division, at any rate in the literary field, between the temper of the greatest American artists and the national temper. The national temper is optimistic, still deeply impressed by the belief in progress and still prone to believe that somewhere a solution can be found, if we try hard enough, for the temporarily distressing human condition. Yet this was not and is not the temper of the most critically esteemed American writers and to be a devoted admirer of Mr. Faulkner, for example, is to be in that degree un-American.

Then there is a division between the more sophisticated artists and the aspiring public that I believe to be greater than in any historical period known to me. Again, this division is not confined to the United States; it is a chasm in all the Western countries. Literature, the visual arts, music, philosophy are all practiced at a high degree of sophistication by highly trained specialists. They are also studied and appreciated by highly sophisticated devotees. But much of the production of the modern artist (using the term in its widest connotation) makes small or no appeal to the average man, not even to the intelligent average man who is conscious that his life would be fuller and better if the arts spoke more loudly to him than they do.

I have said that this division is new. I do not believe that in the thirteenth and fourteenth centuries all the good Catholic worshipers appreciated the scholastic philosophers or fully understood the achievement of Chartres. *The Divine Comedy* and the *Summa* were not popular works or within the reach of everybody. Nor do I believe that all Athenians knew by what divine skill the Parthenon got its proportions or appreciated all that Sophocles meant or were fit to be admitted to the Academy. I could multiply the examples.

But I think the modern situation is different. What a very modern musician means by music or a very modern non-representational artist means by painting or many modern writers mean by literature has only a remote and often invisible connection with what the average sensual man means by these arts. I am aware that public taste has to be educated, that there were people who thought Mozart hard to follow and definitely discordant, that there were people who thought the Impressionists were simply incompetent. Maybe it is going to be like that for all the arts now in such confusion, now cut off, as so often they are, from what used to be their normal audience.

Even if we are all going to make the grade we haven't made it yet, and the average man is tempted, not unreasonably, to throw his hand in. He may exalt the claims of various jazz schools to be art forms as rich as classical music and its heirs or he may deny that classical music has any legitimate heirs. He may see or profess to see in fine camera work the true succession to the great painters, in the engineers the fit heirs of the architects. He may abandon pure literature altogether as a means of spiritual refreshment and turn to history, geography, travel, "know-how" books for more information. If he does so he will be in grave danger of reinforcing in himself the innate American belief that George Santayana commented on, the confidence in quantity, the preference for things that can be measured, the emphasis on more rather than on better, the identification of more *with* better. In our world emphasis on number, on measurable magnitudes, is one of the necessities of life, a necessity that presses ever more hardly on us.

But a life based on a belief that all that should be valued can be measured is like a life based on the belief that all that has to be learned can be taught. It is doomed to emotional sterility and to a sense of deception. Life is not like that and it is painful to find this out too late. What is missing in that life is what I have already alluded to in my remarks on education—the sense of excellence.

The danger to the notion of excellence does not lie only in the irrelevant emphasis on measurable quantity. It can and often does lie in the attribution to mediocrity of the power and prestige of excellence. Here, again at the risk of uttering platitudes, I have to join in the attack on the mass media. For it is possible to argue that they do less harm in their exaltation of the palpably trivial and transitory than in the excessive seriousness with which minor triumphs in the lively arts are greeted. That these lively arts can be diverting I do not deny. So can detective stories, so can much light and some low literature. I do not shudder at a *Saturday Evening Post* cover or wince when I hear of the prices paid for tickets to a fashionable musical.

But a lot of harm is done when a great popular success like *South Pacific* or *My Fair Lady* is puffed up until the distinction between talent and genius is lost sight of, between the work to which one may give the adjective "immortal" with no pedantic scruple and commercial productions of high amusement value that are extremely unlikely to survive the generation that welcomed them. It is not a question of commercial motive. Shakespeare and Molière were both highly commercial men of the theater. It is a question of not giving the rank of a masterpiece to what is simply agreeable, for if you do that you cannot savor the real masterpieces—which is a great loss to the individual and in the aggregate to the national culture. *My Fair Lady* is not *The Marriage of Figaro; By Love Possessed* is not *War and Peace* or *The Ambassadors.*

What I am pleading for is the presentation to the young of the concept that there is such a thing as excellence, that the unexamined life, the emotionally banal life, the life animated by a religion of mere good works and with no philosophy behind it, is inferior to the fuller life of the artist, the philosopher, the saint. And since most of us cannot be any of these things, the next best thing for us is the humble, industrious, and informed admiration for these great achievements of the human spirit.

This is, above all, the function of the universities. To them come a high proportion of the young people who are capable of this initiation. It is against these young people that so much in the modern world—not only in the American modern world but especially in the American modern world—conspires. They need fortification; they need knowledge imparted without pedantry but also without any easy submission to the taste of the hour or the natural laziness of the human mind. The United States has probably never known a period in which its cultural prestige was greater, in literature, in painting, in music, but the achievements that win the respectful interest of the outside world are not those that the mass of the American people (including congressmen in that mass) understand or are likely to understand.

A society that in addition to its immense economic and technical prestige has the prestige of being hospitable to the new, the original, the fruitful in the arts, that welcomes new ideas as well as new gimmicks, has an immense advantage in the contest for men's minds. It is not the novelty of the offerings so much as the possibility of novelty that wins the doubtful faced as an alternative with dogmatism, irrelevant domination of the arts by politics, the regular search for a safe common denominator. There is no such common denominator that is compatible with excellence. The notion of excellence is in this sense undemocratic, but it is not un-American. It was certainly an idea dear to Jefferson and to Lincoln. It will suffice if American public opinion and its official organs remember that "every man hath business and desire such as it is."

American life will be richer and more seductive if it permits and encourages the really exceptional, the really original man to pursue his bent, of course allowing for the fact that there will be phonies and flops at least as often as men of genius or even of remarkable talent. But this waste is one of the luxuries that the United States can now afford. And it must afford it if its way of life is to compete at all levels with that of its rival. It can compete on the technical level (if the United States goes all out). It can compete hands down at the level of popular diversion for, as we know, the iron curtain can hardly keep out American popular music and I suspect that the comics would please millions behind the curtain. But it is not merely as an instrument in the cold war that I urge a bold and possibly offensive insistence on excellence. It is because the great success story of the American people deserves excellence in every human activity.

It would be unworthy of the people who have wrought the American miracle in so many fields to settle for less.

A great triumph of the American spirit would be the fostering of a literary and artistic culture that freely took in all the contributions of its ancestral cultures, confident that to be American is to be not exclusive but welcoming and that Shakespeare and the Bible play a greater part in the making of American culture than Melville, than even Mark Twain. It will be most American when it is most universal.

Epilogue

In recent months the world situation has developed more than it has changed. The United States is still and obviously will remain in competition with the Soviet Union and the terms of the contest have not notably altered. If it is less likely that the contest will terminate in a war of mutual suicide, it is no more likely that the present political status of the world will remain unchanged, that the political habits of 1945 or 1955 will remain suitable without serious alteration for the tests of the coming decade.

Nor will the relative positions of the two great power centers necessarily remain as they are. It is less nonsensical than ever to think it possible (if unlikely) that the Soviet Union's productive capacity will overtake that of the United States. It is highly probable that many of the features of the American economy of abundance will appear inside the Soviet Union and in the satellite countries. It is highly probable that the unceasing technological revolution will make for further similarities between the free world and the rival system and that each side will find itself copying the other or simply going down or up the same road. The ideological rivalry will remain, but it will not improbably be less bitter, less fanatical on each side. At any rate, at this moment of writing the possibility of complete and fairly cheap victory for one side or the other, brought about by internal collapse or a revolutionary change in the balance of terror and power, seems to be getting more and more remote.

The United States is visibly becoming resigned to the reality and the permanence of Soviet power and the rulers of the Soviet Union, increasingly confident that it is technically and economically "over the hump," may be preserved from the worst temptations of fear or of ambition. Political lassitude—which can be observed in Western Europe as well as in the United States—may affect the younger citizens of the Soviet Union for whom the dreams and fears of 1917 are in a remote historical past that they know of only by repute. Crusading for the cause of world revolution may well be as unpopular an activity among the Soviet masses as its converse, crusading for the liberation of Europe (or of Asia), is in the United States or among the peoples of its Western allies. If in different degrees and at different speeds the age of abundance is upon us on both sides of the iron curtain, we shall have to rethink our foreign policy.

The American people who cannot be deposed or will not resign from their position of leadership will have to think harder than recently they have been encouraged to do. They will have to remember that the age of abundance is not yet in sight for the greater part of the human race. The majority of mankind may not be standing on the technical escalator that carries us upward; they may be going backwards; their natural resources may be diminishing; the race between population and resources may go on being lost. If this be so, competition between the two power blocks may be intense in those regions where abundance is still remote, where even "frugal comfort" (to quote Eamon de Valera's ideal for the Irish) may seem a utopian dream. It may not be an affair of rocket sites or military alliances and reversals of alliances. It will certainly be a contest for the hopes, affections and fears of mankind. The great hungry masses of Asia, Africa, and parts of Latin America will have to be fed, and fed in more than a material sense. They will want to be dazzled as well as materially nourished.

In such a world it will not do to laugh off as a mere stunt, as a waste of resources, the great Soviet triumphs in space. Showing mankind, for the first time in its now very long history, the other side of the moon is more than a dazzling feat of technical invention and execution. It is a demonstration of the power of the Soviet society to do things unprecedented in the history of human achievement. If the Russians keep the lead in this conquest of space, this transcendence of human limitations, can we wonder that all over the world tens, even hundreds of millions of men aroused from their millennial resignation will wonder whether it be not true that communism has the key to human progress, that the old "free world" is stagnant and deposed from its fairly recent role of world leadership. Sputniks may not fill men's bellies but they may well fill men's minds.

It does not follow, of course, that the United States should necessarily try to rival the Russians in all they do, should pant after the pacemakers even if certain of overtaking them. But if the race and the game is not to be lost it will be necessary to capture or recapture the imagination of the world. It is almost certainly true that in the advanced societies the "American way of life" is on a seller's market. An abundance of gadgets made desirable by gimmicks, a world of ever-increasing wants if a world of diminishing needs, is the world that all advanced technical societies are entering into or want to enter into. And the rulers of the Soviet world may have to admit many of the promises (and premises) of the capitalist world into their Marxist society. But they need not admit all of them. Looking out on the world that is far from the threshold of abundance, the rulers of Russia may see advantages to be gained not only by such magnificent achievements as the moon shots but by ostentatiously refusing some of the goods the American system provides. The comparative austerity, the imposed puritanism of Russian society may be attractive to the ardent young in the aspiring but desperately poor parts of the world. They may not think that the profit motive is all that a nation needs to pull itself up by its bootstraps. The kind of profit motive with which these societies are familiar may not inspire much moral or practical admiration—and may not deserve to.

Nor is it certain that the picture of American society often innocently and complacently presented to the world by representative American figures wins admiration or respect. That Hollywood should have nothing better to offer Mr. Khrushchev than a shot of *Can-Can* must have reinforced in many minds the vision of the United States as "uncultured," vulgar, greedy, incapable of even perceiving, much less achieving the highest aims of human culture. The bottoms of the girls of the chorus against "the glimpses of the moon"? It is an unfair parallel but not an implausible one.

Marxism in Russia has led to such stifling of the human spirit, such coerced obedience, and such crippling of artistic creation that it is easy to forget that in its heyday it promised a liberation of the human spirit from the mere crippling bonds of economic necessity and proposed the creation or, better, the revelation of a new man, developing for the first time in history all the potentialities of man which earlier historical systems had necessarily frustrated. That this utopian vision is utopian, that the old Adam will survive the formal liberation that communism promises, I firmly believe. It is true that the vision can be and has been used to dazzle and deceive, used as an instrument of exploitation no less odious than that attributed to capitalism by the Marxist prophets. But we are faced with a world in which the vision still has power to dazzle and will certainly dazzle if the American people and the American state have no more to offer the eager, angry, uncritical young leaders of the new nations than more and more supermarkets.

In the new, formally peaceful contest in which the United States is engaged, originality of mind, tolerance and understanding of the problems of other peoples, and a feeling for splendor as well as for plenty are among the most important weapons. But they cannot simply be commanded and exported. If they are not encouraged to grow at home, if the climate of American opinion, the temper of American life is dominated by the ideal of more and more consumer goods, with the quality of life assumed to be measurable in terms of the greatest aggregate of such goods, then the battle for the minds of men will be lost. For it is unlikely that the United States can give the majority of mankind, now, the key to the storehouse of plenty; even if she could, it might not avail her unless she could give dreams and visions as well.

Of course, it is not only to enable the United States to compete in the outside world that the ideal of democratic excellence should be preached and practiced. The American people deserve better—and want better—than a paradise of rapidly obsolete usable goods. To deny this is not only to condemn the United States to political defeat in the outside world but to make that world easily open to the conviction that the defeat is deserved. Therefore, everything in the interior life of the United States that reinforces the interior or exterior caricature of the American way of life—from rigged quiz programs upward—is dangerous in this world spinning "down the ringing grooves of change" at an unprecedented speed. The values of the market place are not to be despised, but they are not universally valid. And it is certain that no nation that has no other values can hope to lead or to be secure. That way Carthage went.

But the contest for the mind and heart of the world has not gone, is not going all one way. The generosity of the United States and of its people has not been unnoticed, even though the belief that the generosity was based exclusively on military and economic calculation of advantage has at times had a dangerous plausibility. But the great success of American policy, the salvation of Western Europe, has not only saved that treasure house from passing into the Soviet orbit but has made possible the reconstruction of a great economic power that in its turn is capable (if adequately led) of doing its part in saving the poorer regions of the world from despair and its temptations.

The United States is less than ever the autocratic paymaster of states only formally independent and now knows both the gratifications and the irritations of having as allies countries with both the will and the means to insist on serious consideration of their point of view. To adjust to the new role may be difficult for the American people and the American government, but the economic and political conditions that make the new role necessary are a reinforcement of the American side in the world competition that could not have been anticipated when General Marshall made his famous offer in 1947.

Nor is everything outside Europe bound to go against American interests and sentiments. The forces of often irrational nationalism that can be and have been both irritating and obstructive work also against an easy "take-over" by the Soviet Union. The competition for the favors of the new or resurrected nations of Asia and Africa is not necessarily in itself a bad thing. Though it would be absurdly optimistic to foresee, in any visible future, a genuine cooperation between the Western and the Soviet bloc in the rescuing of the impoverished masses of the world from their miserable condition, it would be narrowly selfish and timorous to see in every example of Soviet aid to a backward economy a defeat for the West. It need not be that and if the aid does in fact benefit the people involved it would be churlish and foolish merely to lament the political gains that the Soviet Union *may*—not necessarily *will*—secure by skillfully applied generosity. (After all, the numerous Americans who complain that the United States has not been able to buy friends by her generosity might reflect that this may be true for the Soviet Union too.)

The nearly universal belief in the politically minded classes of the great colored majority of the world that the old imperialist powers could do and meant to do no good and that their successor in wickedness or selfishness was the United States, is not so universal in 1959 as it was even as recently as 1958. "The spirit of Bandung," which was to unite the colored helots of the world against their quondam masters, is not so potent as it was. For one thing, the new nations, regrettably but naturally, have managed to acquire enemies nearer home. Nationalism seems condemned to do this wherever it triumphs. For another, the educational experience of the realities of "freedom" is not totally wasted. It is beginning to dawn on the less rhetorically minded of national leaders that slogans are not adequate solutions for desperately urgent economic and social problems. Even if it is still believed that the problems are the result of imperialism, the fact remains that they have survived the end of empire. And the United States, only partly and only recently tarred with the imperialist brush, is in a position to aid with tact and patience—and money—some of the nations struggling not to be free but to give a concrete meaning to freedom. The American people will contract themselves out of this opportunity and duty at their peril.

The duty will not be easy to fulfill. It is as true now as it has been ever since 1945 that there are areas in which the exercise of American wisdom, power and generosity is difficult, regions in which the exercise of Russian power and cunning is easy. Afghanistan is an example. There are regions in which the old and tried nationalist device of finding or inventing an enemy to account for the failure of the revolution to deliver the goods works to the disadvantage of the United States. Cuba and Argentina are examples. There may be regions in which an effective and consistent policy is difficult to find and nearly impossible to apply. The Middle East is an example. In short, no more now than in the past are the American people wise in expecting quick and final and easy success everywhere. For a generation much less brilliant and universal success will have to be sought with intelligence, resolution and generosity—and thankfully received.

It is possible to be alarmed about the immediate future of areas in which the American power of action is limited and where history is possibly being made too fast, as in Africa. Who knows what will be the state or the status of the Congo a year from now? Who knows how long some of the new states and federations will stay united? Too great an expectation of quick and easy progress, leading to quick and sour disappointment, is a danger that confronts the American people as they look outward on a world that in many regions, if not in all, "they never made."

Again, the turbulent current of history does not run all one way. How much the face of Asia changed in 1959 when it was revealed even to the most hopeful, the most credulous, the most color-conscious, that imperialism need not wear a white skin! How quickly the astronomical boasts of economic progress made by the Chinese government proved false! Perhaps Tibet and the stumblings and retreats of the forward march of Chinese Communism cancel out for the moment the impressive accuracy of Russian rocketry! Perhaps the Indians and the Burmese care less for the moon than for what is being done inside China—and outside China! At any rate, the old illusion of automatic peace, cooperation and good will among all the nations of "Asia" is dead. Even the reality of the conception of "Asia" may be questioned by the more sophisticated.

It would of course be an error of the first magnitude to see in the divisions, contradictions, failures and retreats of the rulers of China the ending of the Chinese Communist experiment or the imminent return of the Chinese people to the good old ways. For better or for worse, what is going on in China is in scale and possibly in historical importance the greatest experiment in human history. It cannot be reduced to a mere matter of being "pro- or anti-Western," in this case Western always meaning American. With whatever regrets or resentment the American people will have to accept, as the Russian government will have to accept, the appearance of China on the world's stage as at least the equal of the two great world powers of today. It will require imagination and magnanimity to digest this formidable fact and wisdom, patience and power to cope with it.

We can be certain that the world will change in many novel and disconcerting ways in the next decade. We can be certain, too, that the contest for survival in independence will take new forms—some are already visible as the rulers of Russia assert, and I believe assert with sincerity, their ability to compete with the United States in the organization of abundance for a world that has desperate need of it. To deal with that rapidly changing world the American people will need to show flexibility of means if not of ends, readiness to look unpleasant realities in the face, resignation to the fact that their destiny is totally enmeshed with that of the whole human race as that race stands on the edge of space. Many comfortable and, in their day, rational and useful beliefs and habits will have to be scrapped.

Many useful and defensible principles of action, such as the belief that "the business of the United States is business," will have to be demoted from universal rules of conduct to being part of the necessary wisdom of the American people, who have more things to worry about and more aims to attain than business or business success. And for a long time, when the people would naturally rather relax, they will be forced—if they are adequately led—to gaze outward, since they have lost forever the right of total reliance on "that inward eye which is the bliss of solitude."

The days of going it alone are over. There must be a continual recollection of the deep truth enshrined in the text "righteousness exalteth a nation" and much that is tolerable in the national life seen from the inside may seem a dangerous luxury or abdication seen from the outside. Preaching is easy, but is there any more important task for the leaders of America than to believe and to act as if they believed with Lincoln that "right makes might; and in that faith let us to the end, dare to do our duty as we understand it"?